HOW
TO SELL
LIKE A
NATURAL
BORN
SALES-
PERSON

Learn How the Best Make Success Look Easy!

DR. GARY S. GOODMAN

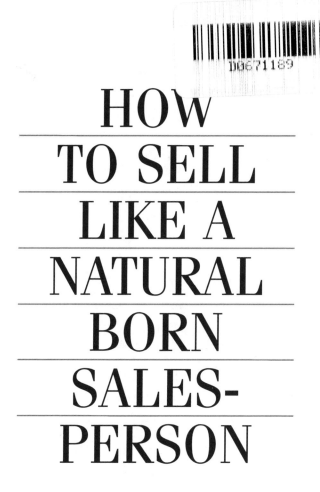

Adams Media Corporation
HOLBROOK, MASSACHUSETTS

Dedication

To my wife, colleague, and best friend, Dr. Deanne Goodman;
To our wonderful daughter, Amanda Leigh; and
To the warm memory of my father, Bernard Goodman.

Acknowledgments

I would like to thank Jessica Wainwright, my agent from the Literary Group International, and Ed Walters, my publisher at Adams Media, for their efforts to bring this book into the world.

I would also like to express my gratitude to my consulting clients and to you, the reader.

Published by Adams Media Corporation
260 Center Street, Holbrook, MA 02343

ISBN: 1-58062-051-5

Printed in the United States of America.

J   I   H   G   F   E   D   C   B   A

Library of Congress Cataloging-in-Publication Data
Goodman, Gary S.
How to sell like a natural born salesperson / by Gary S. Goodman.
p.   cm.
Includes index.
ISBN 1-58062-051-5
1. Selling. I. Title.
HF5438.25.G6598   1998
658.8'1—dc21   98-19296
                          CIP

This book is available at quantity discounts for bulk purchases.
For information, call 1-800-872-5627 (in Massachusetts, 781-767-8100).

Visit our home page at http://www.adamsmedia.com

CONTENTS

INTRODUCTION

When I was just breaking into advertising sales, something out of the ordinary happened. A hefty guy ambled into the sales bullpen. He could have been King Midas for all I knew. Gold adorned his outsized neck, wrists, and fingers.

"Who is this guy?" I murmured, as he methodically opened his super-chic, soft-sided briefcase. He retrieved only three manila folders from it, which he ceremoniously fanned across his desk. His manicured fingers selected a single folder, which he communed with for a few moments.

He seemed like a muscled version of Minnesota Fats, the legendary pool player who Jackie Gleason played in *The Hustler*. Through mental telepathy, the boss seemed to detect this fellow's presence.

The only overt acknowledgment the boss made of the salesman was a slow smile that creased his face. It was a sly, self-satisfied grin that signaled, this is going to be *good*.

The Big Man lightly dialed the phone and started to speak. I expected a deep voice to bellow out, but I was wrong. If he had been a singer, he wouldn't have been a bass or a baritone as his physique suggested.

He was a tenor, a telephonic Luciano Pavarotti, who was about to Reach Out & Sell Someone®.

He called Coca-Cola and spoke to an executive secretary as if he were soothing a kitty. No fast moves, just a politely purred overture.

His personality shifted when the prospect came onto the line. His voice expressed authority and self-assurance. Within two minutes, this strictly-business superstar had popped one whopper of a sale.

He paused less than a nanosecond before rhythmically dialing the phone again. This time he called Capitol Records. Same sequence as the first call. Another big sale.

He wrote a few notes on his folders, and then he slowly got up from his seat and handed them to our secretary who nodded her head and smiled the same smile she ordinarily reserved only for the boss. Then, the salesman collected his briefcase and keys and quietly glided out the door.

One of my buddies, who was as astonished as I, broke the silence with these reverential words:

"Elvis has left the theater."

Later, the boss came out, asked the secretary something, and seemed deeply satisfied by her reply. What I discovered later was the fact that the Big Man had earned about $1,000 in commissions, in approximately a half hour of selling. Of course, he had made even more for the company.

I came to realize that this was his standard routine. He'd drive his Porsche down from the Hollywood Hills once or twice a week, hit a few home runs, then retire to get some rays by his pool.

He was one of the first natural born salespeople I worked with in my career.

The first natural born salesperson I ever knew was my Dad. He was a sales champ everywhere he worked. It didn't matter if he was selling radio advertising or lining up investors to produce TV programs. By temperament and capabilities, he was the classical natural.

He could have written the cowboy tune, "Don't Fence Me In," because he liked to be given lots of room in which to maneuver. He was the opposite of what corporations regard as a team player. He was his own person through and through, and his productivity was so strong that he pulled the weight of several people.

Naturally, he hated the entire idea of being regimented, and for most of his life he even refused to wear a watch. "Rules," he observed, "are for other people, Gary. I do things MY WAY, and it has always worked out."

Once, he was given a sales award by a pump company where he had pumped up sales to unprecedented levels. Dad was urged to share some of his success secrets with his less successful peers at a national sales meeting.

Although he demurred, his manager insisted. "Just tell them how you rose to the top, Bernie."

Oh, did he tell them!

"Ladies and gentlemen, I'll be brief. Do you see that clock on the wall? I don't, because it's meaningless to me.

"You've probably heard that 'The Early Bird Gets The Worm,' and that's a fact. But that's ALL he gets—WORMS! Nobody ever made a dime by waking-up early. We make money by making sales. And the way to make sales is to feel good, first.

"I'll tell you how I make myself feel good. I'm a night owl, so I wake up at 8:30 or at 9:00 in the morning. I shower, dress, and go buy myself a nice, big breakfast. I may make a few phone calls, and in the afternoon I'll visit some prospects.

"And if I don't feel like selling on a given day, I won't. That is how I made it to the top. Thank you very much."

Most people would love to deliver a radical speech like that once in their lives just to see the reaction. But my Dad, and millions of natural born salespeople, actually walk the walk, and talk the talk.

They're mavericks, and they don't mind saying so. But they also do seven very significant things that I'll reveal to you in this book. Some of the most intellectual salespeople are aware of their techniques, but most naturals don't fit into this category.

As a rule, naturals are either ignorant of their techniques, or they deliberately obscure them so their managers won't be able to clone them, and their associates won't rival them. My Dad refused to do his telephone prospecting and appointment setting at the office because he didn't want anyone to hear his secret techniques.

For naturals, selling is super easy. It's a closely guarded fact, because if it were known that they don't sweat bullets worrying about who they're going to sell, or how they're going to "pitch" them, their bosses would probably try to cut their salaries or commissions. Nike might say that natural born salespeople Just Do It.

And what's especially interesting to me, as a consultant, salesperson, and communication theorist is the fact that many naturals are unaware of what they do that garners them such great results. Surely, if you ask them what techniques they use, they'll reply with something that seems to make sense.

"I just try to be my customers' friend," they'll say. But if you press them, they'll come up short on specifics.

"How do you act friendly?"

"What do you mean?" they'll wonder.

"Do you do anything special?"

"Nope, I just try to be myself."

And it's that phrase that is so revealing. They say, "I just try to BE." This means they don't separate who they ARE from what they DO. This enables them to consistently succeed.

But we don't have to be at a loss to understand and exploit the secrets of natural born salespeople. After having trained and coached thousands of salespeople who work in the field as well as on the phone, I can honestly tell you that natural born salespeople DO certain critical things that cause them to be successful.

They also have a great time selling, and so can you.

You can unleash the natural born salesperson who lies dormant inside of you. Even if you think you AREN'T like them and that they possess unique gifts, you can ACT as they do and produce great results.

All you need to do is to read the following chapters. I'll provide you with all the specifics you'll need to become transformed from either a nonsalesperson, or from an underachieving salesperson, into a dynamic, capable, and fun-loving professional.

I've pulled it off, for myself. This is why I know it'll work for you, too.

But there's a trick to it. You have to know what to emulate and what to leave alone—otherwise you could pick up some wasteful habits.

Here is an overview of the seven secrets of natural born salespeople:

1. *They develop high self-esteem and always feel they deserve the sale.*

2. *They create instant credibility and immediate rapport with their prospects.*
3. *They get customers to sell themselves.*
4. *They use passion and powerful emotions in selling customers.*
5. *They persuade through the effective use of body language.*
6. *They multiply their impact by mastering several sales media while never wasting their time.*
7. *They turn lemons into lemonade by transforming every setback, rejection, and slump into a major advantage.*

Do you want to make great money and have a ton of fun while you do it? Buckle up, because your next stop is sales greatness!

CHAPTER 1

FALL
IN LOVE
WITH
YOURSELF!

You're pretty terrific. Did you know that?

Natural born salespeople start with this assumption about themselves. If they were lucky, it was imbued into their psyches by doting parents and relatives who made it seem the world revolved around their little wards.

In many cases, the realization of our self-worth comes later. If you aspire to selling like naturals sell, an unshakable sense of self-worth and self-love must become embedded into your mind and your soul. You have to convince yourself that you're well beyond okay, or all right. You're out-and-out tremendous.

If you believe this to your core, right now, this chapter will serve as a good reinforcement.

My purpose is to show you how to project a sense of easy comfort with yourself and self assurance that tells prospects you're a secure person—someone they can count on, and buy from, with confidence.

By the time you've finished with this chapter, I hope you'll be nearly bursting with a sense that you deserve the best of everything. Because you do deserve the best!

The Positive Connection Between Self-Esteem and Earnings

I have important news for you. You'll earn sales and the big money that natural born salespeople earn *when you feel you deserve it and you convince your prospects to feel the same way about you.*

Deserving isn't simply a result of making a customer feel grateful for all of your attention and concern. That would imply that there is an objective standard that prospects consult before deciding to award us with their business. Many buying decisions aren't based upon any such arithmetic.

It's not like sellers can say, "I really put myself out for you, Mr. Prospect. Now, it's time to reward me with my commission!" Prospects won't respond positively to that approach. As one savvy attorney mused, "The half-life of a client's gratitude can be measured in minutes," even if you've done a dandy job.

Case in Point: Ad Agency Selling

Just look at what Jill has to go through to earn a new client in her advertising agency business. If she wants to score with a big-name athletic shoe company, which routinely injects megabucks into TV, radio, billboards, and print media, she's going to have to generate an elaborate pitch just to be in the running for the big prize.

She knows that big clients also insist that she WOW them with a presentation of what she intends to do for them. This multimedia spectacular, which could run into the tens-of-thousands of dollars, is done on spec.

According to ad agency customs, she can't pass along her costs to the potential client. This means that the shoe company can listen to her ideas, politely smile, and then leave with a certain number of her ideas. For FREE!

Does Jill DESERVE a sale because she worked s-o-o-o hard? You may think so, and I may sympathize, but in the real world of client thinking the answer isn't NO—it's HECK NO! They don't feel they owe her, or us, anything.

Deserving Starts with You

Deserving the sale really starts inside of you. It is first and foremost a frame of mind—an expectation that naturals project. *You must feel deserving to earn big sales and big bucks.*
Now, don't get me wrong. I'm not telling you to seem NEEDY. You don't want to come across as if you HAVE TO HAVE THE ORDER OR YOU WON'T EAT. If NEEDINESS or DESPERA-TION come through as signals to your prospects, then you'll scare away business.

By deserving, I mean that you should project the impression that *this customer should belong to you and to nobody else.* It's as if you OWN the client, the second you come into contact with each other.

By looking at you, or by hearing your voice on the telephone, the prospect should feel that you have the strongest possible expec-tation that she is going to leave your presence having bought, or at least having committed, to making substantial progress toward reaching an understanding.

Naturals Don't Believe in Looky-Lou's!

Realtors have a favorite term for people who drive around on Sunday afternoon hitting every garage sale and stopping at every open house they can find, supposedly because they have nothing else to do. Because they say they're just looking, these folks are commonly referred to as Looky-Lou's.

Naturals don't believe there are such creatures on our beau-tiful, blue planet as Looky-Lou's. Naturals, at least in their ini-tial encounters, believe every person who is in their closing zone, whether that is a living room or an auto showroom, is a *bona fide* buyer.

Here's their logic. Do most adults deliberately waste their time if they have ZERO interest in buying? No way! They're at least somewhat rational about how they allocate their personal resources, and they know that there is only so much time that they'll be able to smell the roses before the big show is over.

Naturals figure that a person who says he's just looking is really doing a lot more than that. At the very least, he's *curious about what he's looking at.*

Possibly, he wants to see the new car models that have just arrived around October first. Are they as sleek and efficient and luxurious as the commercials say? Are they going to set the imports on their ears?

Certainly, Joe Smith may not have stopped at the Chevy dealership for the purpose of buying a new car or truck, but his curiosity can ripen into serious interest if he is treated right and if he's provided a rationale for buying.

Most critical is the attitude of the salesperson. If she doesn't treat the prospect as if he's just an inch away from becoming a buyer, why should the prospect regard himself that way?

Oh, Did I Blow It Once

Speaking of the auto business, I used to lease cars for a living. I was a mere pup of twenty when I started out, but the business gave me a great sales education.

One of my more stinging lessons came at the hands of a couple of eighteen-year-olds. This young pair of lovebirds came into our Beverly Hills leasing center, and it was my turn to handle the walk-ins so I invited them to my cubicle.

No sooner did we sit down than the young man said, "I'd like to lease a Ferrari, and also something a little less nice (ha-ha) for my girlfriend!"

Sure, kid, sure . . . In your dreams. That's what I thought, and I had to suppress a huge guffaw, because I thought these pee-wees were really wasting my time. I asked the young gent to fill out a credit application, and I told him I'd phone him with the "results."

I stood up, smiled, and dispatched him with a handshake, and a moment later they were out the door. Of course, I figured his application would be turned down in a heartbeat by our tough-as-nails credit manager, Tony. Did I have a surprise coming!

Tony nearly tap danced into my office. Uncharacteristically jubilant, he looked like a Fred Astaire or Gene Kelly wind-up toy.

"Where is he?" Tony chirped, while scanning the entire sales floor for my errant prospects.

"Who?" I blurted back.

"Your customer, Mr. Hawkins and his fiancee."

"Oh, you mean THOSE KIDS?"

"Yeah, the trust fund baby and his bride-to-be."

"You mean he has money?" I asked, as the blood drained from my face.

"Money?" Tony laughed. "He's worth *millions*! Lease him anything he wants—his girlfriend, too. Just make sure he co-signs for her, okay?"

You can imagine how I spent the better part of that afternoon and the next morning. I dialed like a madman, leaving messages for young MR. HAWKINS everywhere. Finally, he gave me the courtesy of calling back to inform me that he had leased his cars from the local Ferrari dealership.

What's the moral to the story? Don't judge a book by its cover? Partly, but it's more important than that. If you want to win like a natural born salesperson:

Expect every prospect to buy!

Prospects deserve our respect, and you'll find that by projecting a serious selling interest in them you'll coax to the surface a serious buying interest from them. Otherwise, they might blow you off just as I did with that couple.

Don't Play I'm Not Okay, You're Not Okay

For years afterwards, I pondered the selling errors I made with those young folks. Why did I rush to judge his spending capabilities? Sure, he was young, and the probabilities were on my side that he was over his head in even thinking about a Ferrari.

As you know, I was dead wrong. Looking back upon that scene now, I can see where I REALLY went wrong. I have to admit that I was probably just a little bit jealous of this kid who was even younger than I was. He thought nothing of breezing in and asking for the best we could offer.

I think I was threatened by that, in part, because I thought I was doing pretty well to be driving one of the company's plain vanilla cars that were kept for account executives. I was struggling to pay my rent and to advance in my new career, and here was a KID who had it all. He started life on third base and thought he had hit a triple!

I probably didn't want to believe he could afford to lease the sports car. Fundamentally, I resented him.

And underneath that emotion was an even more disabling one: I didn't think I deserved a Ferrari, either. So, I was just projecting my lack of self-worth upon this youthful multimillionaire.

Psychologically, I suppose I was saying:

"I don't deserve a car like this, so neither do you!"

Which is the equivalent of shouting out:

"I'm not okay, and you're not okay, either!"

That is a lose-lose relationship message. You might see this scenario as highly nutty and exceedingly unusual. But it isn't.

Salespeople with low self-esteem blow sales all the time, and they're not at all in touch with why they failed. In fact, they usually blame their prospects when things don't go their way.

But the true culprit is really their low self-esteem.

Do You Deserve to Be Rich?

Does wanting to be rich have anything to do with selling like a natural born salesperson? Absolutely.

Most naturals believe they deserve to make a great living and that they are entitled to drive great cars, live in wonderful neighborhoods, and enjoy regular luxury vacations.

They suffer from zero MONEY GUILT. There isn't a socialistic bone in their bodies. They want and feel that they should have the biggest slice of cake and the best end of each and every deal.

When they walk into a restaurant, their eyes scan the room for the best dining locations, and they tell the hosts or hostesses exactly where they wish to be seated. Does it matter that two dozen people put their names in before they arrived?

In a word, no. They don't care about FAIRNESS, except when it comes to getting their fair share of salaries, commissions, or bonuses. The words, *You'll just have to wait your turn*, are fighting words to naturals.

If you're thinking, "Gee, I don't like people who act that way," I can tell you one important thing. THEY DON'T CARE WHAT YOU THINK, UNLESS YOU ARE A BUYER. If you're a bystander, or just another civilian, you're irrelevant.

On the other hand, you might admire, openly or secretly, their nerve. If so, you have a much better chance of emulating them and getting more of life's rewards in return.

But to qualify for the bigger money, you have to tell yourself that you deserve it. Let me convince you that you do.

There's More than Enough Money to Go Around

Unlike the Ferrari-leasing couple, very few people grow up awash in money. They don't have a twelve-car garage with live-in butlers and maids. Sadly, most folks grow up in homes that feel much, much poorer.

Mike Todd, the famous movie producer, once said, "I've never been poor, but I have been broke." Being broke, he pointed out, is a temporary condition; being poor is a debilitating frame of mind that can last a lifetime, if we allow it.

But we don't have to let it last another minute. The first thing you should start telling yourself is:

There's enough money and wealth to go around.

You may not have enough in your pocket to convince you of this fact, but please bear with me for a minute.

When I was studying for my M.B.A. at the Claremont Graduate School, I took a class on money and banking, and it was a real eye-opener. We learned that there are many, many forms of money.

There's cash, of course, and there's money in the nation's checking accounts. There are money market funds, as well as credit lines that provide money to fund charge cards and loans. There are interbank deposits, and the list goes on and on.

A recent article in the *Los Angeles Times* asserted that individuals and institutions from many nations are pouring money into our country because they can get a better return on their funds. So we not only have our own money, but we have much of the excess money belonging to the rest of the world!

And do you know what happens at regular intervals through the Federal Reserve Board? They EXPAND THE MONEY SUPPLY by printing more ones, fives, twenties, hundreds, and thousand-dollar bills.

Why do they do that? They do it to keep the economy humming along, so we'll never run out of the green stuff!

The trick is to get more of that money to flow through us. Natural born salespeople overcome one of the most powerfully restricting thoughts that the impoverished entertain: there isn't enough to go around.

There is no scarcity of money. Please get that firmly fixed in your mind, because once you believe it, you can make the next adjustment to tell yourself that you deserve to have more come your way.

Vanquish Your Money Myths and You'll Attract More Money

First, you need to vanquish the money myths that you're probably running around with. But, you might wonder, why should you get rid of them?

Here's the reason:

If you're hostile towards money, you'll scare it away. And if you're ambivalent about it, you certainly won't amass much of it, nor will you keep it for any significant length of time.

Let's begin the process of changing our thinking for the better by slaying the biggest of all money myths:

Money is the root of all evil.

First of all, it's just plain false. Money, by itself, is nothing but a medium of exchange and a storehouse of value. It is a way of measuring the value you have tendered to others in our society through your labor and your investments.

It can be used to beautify the highways, as they do in Texas (one of my favorite states). Each year, the Department of Highways plants thousands and thousands of bluebonnets.

Or, money can be misused to plant heroin-producing poppies in Colombia. The choices we make in spending our money are critical in determining money's effectiveness, but by itself, the green stuff is completely neutral.

One TV evangelist, used to regularly proclaim: "Money isn't the root of all evil. The ABSENCE of money is the root of all evil!"

Several Biblical scholars have pointed out that the Good Book really says it's the LOVE of money, to the exclusion of loving ourselves, other people, and goodness itself that is really at the root of evil.

But let me say this: If you don't at least feel friendly towards money, you're not going to attract a goodly amount of it. You should be honest with yourself and admit that earning and sustaining a big income is a major life goal, and it's a goal worth feeling GREAT about!

You simply won't provide yourself with enough motivation if you tell yourself, "Gee, I'd LIKE to have a bigger paycheck," or "It would be NICE if I had more extra money to spend."

Be assertive when it comes to thinking about money. PLAN to earn much more of it, and set your INCOME EXPECTATIONS higher and higher.

Tell yourself:

"Every day, in every way, I'm growing richer and richer!"

You'll Earn (Only) What You Have to Earn

I know many successful sales managers who have echoed one sentiment:

Show me a salesperson who has a BIG NUT TO CRACK each and every month, and I'll show you a great salesperson!

What do they mean? They know that salespeople have a SET POINT, just as all folks are reputed to have when it comes to body weight.

Nutritionists say that if we try to reduce our weight through crash dieting, we'll instantly gain it back because our metabolisms operate to maintain certain equilibrium levels or set weight points. Unless we change these set points through sensible dieting and additional exercising, we'll remain at our weight levels and not improve.

The same concept applies to selling. Natural born salespeople give themselves very high set points. They aspire to, and try to maintain, standards of living that are way beyond those of average salespeople.

Some naturals insist upon buying themselves a new luxury car every year or two. Or, they trade up the houses they live in for better digs every three to five years. And they're always on the lookout for the very, very best in vacation venues.

Put all of this together and you have a salesperson who JUST CAN'T ALLOW HIS SALES TO SLIP. And he doesn't, because he knows exactly how many orders he needs to write up to make his big nut each week, month, or year.

And one more thing: Naturals simply refuse to go backward.

You Have to Love Yourself to Feel You Deserve Prosperity

I believe, as do most naturals, that prosperity is our birthright. We weren't put on this beautiful and wealthy planet to be deprived.

If you honestly love certain people, whether they're friends, family, or neighbors, you probably celebrate when they achieve wonderful things.

In other words, you want good things for them. Why? Because you appreciate them.

If so, why is it that so many of us feel it's okay for others to prosper, but somehow it's wrong if we directly seek that outcome for ourselves? Some folks delude themselves into believing that it's more moral, or spiritual for us to suffer while others thrive.

I just don't buy this concept of self-effacement. We should build ourselves up, each and every day, and teach ourselves to enjoy and expect to reap this wonderful world's bounty.

Does this mean we want it all for ourselves like modern day Midases? Absolutely not. I think it's nearly impossible to extract top value from life without giving back top value in return.

Earning Big Incomes Is a Win-Win Proposition

When we seek the best for ourselves, it is a win-win proposition for everyone. If you want proof of this precept, just look at today's batch of billionaires.

Bill Gates, founder and head of Microsoft, is reputed to own assets valued at about forty billion dollars. I know that there are millions of folks who will read this statistic and proclaim that *nobody* should be worth all that money!

I beg to differ. First of all, he is one of the key people who has revolutionized productivity around the world during the past twenty years. Unquestionably, he is responsible for building a large part of today's computer software industry, as well as for helping the companies of the world to increase their output by trillions of dollars. (I'm composing this book, using one of his word processing programs!)

In my mind, he has been compensated quite fairly for his contribution. I say this for a very practical reason. If I devise a way to do what he has done in my own field, I'd like to earn just as much. So I'm the last person on earth who wants to shrink the rewards for others.

Because as long as they're free to do it, so am I! I don't resent them. If anything, I openly admire them, and so should you.

That's what naturals do, because they feel they deserve the best for themselves. Why shouldn't others feel the exact same way about themselves? What goes around comes around, right?

I'm fairly confident that Mr. Gates loves himself. If he didn't, he'd be incapable of rewarding himself with a fifty million dollar house filled with fine art and the latest in electronic gadgetry.

Please Repeat after Me: I Deserve Success, I Deserve Success

I urge you to start keeping an inspiration file. You can start by putting certain phrases and ideas into your computer, or carry them with you on a notepad or in a daily planner. Access these upbeat notions daily to psych yourself up.

You can find bits of inspiration and self-esteem builders nearly everywhere. I'll give you a boost by sharing those that I find particularly motivating. By repeating these statements, I elevate my self-esteem and get energized. They prepare me to sell like a natural. And I'm sure they'll work for you.

Select the ones you like, and try to repeat at least a few of them every day before you see prospects or attempt to sell anyone. Here are twenty-two of my favorites, along with brief explanations as to what they mean and what they'll do to help you to sell like a natural.

1. *Today, I'm going to give 100 percent.* I like this statement because it forces me to commit to excellence and to not hold anything back. Without making an explicit commitment to going all out, we can fall into the bad habit of cruising through supposed downtimes such as lunch hours and late afternoon hours.

2. *The present is my moment of power.* This is a great statement because it swiftly slices away the past. It doesn't matter if the last five prospects all slammed their doors in your face. Stop thinking about that! It's already over. The present is your point of power, not the past. Take full advantage of it.

3. *I can produce the results I want in my life, exactly the way I want to produce them.* I like this one because it says I don't have to become a crowd pleaser in order to succeed. Find a formula that works for you and stick to it. It's what coaches tell pitchers who are suddenly in the World Series: Go with the pitches that got you here.

4. *Selling is a creative act.* I'm going to have fun with it! I subscribe to the idea that there's something wrong with our approach to selling if it feels like unrelenting drudgery. Naturals insist upon having a good time. They transform work into play.

One way they do this is turning selling functions into games. One game is to see how many prospects I can cold call in the next hour. They may even keep mental records of their personal best scores, and then try to beat them.

They can even offer themselves contests with neat incentives. "If I close two deals this morning, I'm going to the beach this afternoon!"

5. *I control the results I get.* This statement is not only true, but it precludes us from whining about how bad luck is descending upon us, or how others are frustrating our efforts. By insisting that

we're in charge of our outcomes, we'll empower ourselves to succeed at each and every moment.

6. *I have unlimited potential.* I think one of the most debilitating feelings we can have is being trapped within a certain low performance cycle. This usually occurs when we settle for less by assuming that we can only reach a limited level of achievement, and that higher ranges aren't realistic to strive for.

As a sales manager and consultant, I have delighted in rebutting this limiting belief by hiring novices who kick the butts of veteran salespeople who have fallen into complacency. It's amazing to see what happens when a prior limitation is suddenly lifted.

For years, no runner had broken the four-minute mile, despite the fact that thousands had tried. Roger Bannister came along and clocked in under that magical marker, and suddenly scores of his fellow athletes did the same once they were convinced it was possible and realistic.

Keep telling yourself that you have unlimited potential, because this message won't usually come from other people who are beset with their own limitations.

7. *My performance follows my beliefs.* If I believe I can do it, I probably can do it. And if I believe I can't, I probably can't do it. This is a fundamental law of success. If we want to achieve at higher levels, we need to formulate beliefs about our capabilities that will fit the new circumstances we wish to create.

8. *No negative beliefs can be inflicted upon me that I do not consciously accept.* We all know people who try to tell us what is good for us and impose certain limitations upon us. Very often, they can't see success for themselves, so they definitely don't see it for us.

When you're aspiring to higher levels in life, these toxic personalities consult a Geiger counter that tells them that you're in the midst of doing some serious changing for the better. Typically, they swoop down to trip you up just as you're about to become airborne.

Recognize them for the party poopers that they are, and don't allow yourself to accept their limited definitions of you. You can avoid them, physically, by putting distance between yourself and them. Or you can dispute their assessments of you and try to convince them that a "new you" is taking over.

Generally, I've found that the distancing method is better. If you stop to persuade them of your changes, they'll just have more provocation to try to stop you by filling you with self-doubts. Better to put some highway between yourselves than to listen to that junk.

9. *I respect my genius.* Most of us are smarter than we give ourselves credit for. If you have a breakthrough idea as to how you can increase sales or customer satisfaction, by all means, give it a try.

Don't make the mistake of feeling that you have to run everything by a committee before taking action. You can second guess yourself so many times that you come to severely doubt the wisdom in the new plan you devised.

I broke in the leasing business by making cold calls over the phone. My manager noticed what I was doing and he said, "Nobody makes it in this business by cold calling over the phone, Gary. You have to hit the pavement and see people."

I disagreed, and to his credit, he let me stick to my plan. A few days after he told me it was impossible, I not only leased my first car, but my second as well to the same cold called prospect.

Within a week, my sales manager became a convert. He made it a rule that all new salespeople work on the phones first before being allowed to go out into the field.

10. *Nothing is impossible for me.* I don't know whether it was my fault or that of my teachers, but I came out of high school believing that I was lousy at math. It's true that I got low grades in Algebra, but I was never sure why this was the case.

As I matured, I found I used math all the time in business, and I actually discovered I have a good aptitude for numbers. (The minute dollar signs were attached to numbers my abilities soared!) When I was opening some very old papers, I discovered some of my elementary school report cards.

Guess what? Throughout primary school I received EXCELLENT grades in arithmetic. It was only in a few classes that I underachieved, and so I have adjusted my beliefs in my own abilities. Now I take special glee in tracking my investments, and I have an uncanny ability to remember, and exploit, the pricing histories of stocks and mutual funds!

Now I believe nothing is impossible for me, and my current math ability is a testament to that idea.

11. *I expect to win.* Life is a self-fulfilling prophecy. If you expect to win, usually, you will. And if you expect to lose, count on it happening with disturbing regularity.

My favorite football team, the Trojans of the University of Southern California had their second miserable season in a row.

During the season, the coach announced that the team was in crisis. No kidding! Everyone in the country knows that U.S.C. has tremendous athletes on the field, but there is something else that is killing their performance.

They don't expect to win.

It's just that simple. Games that should be poundings in their favor, are all too close until the final minutes expire from the clock. Even in victory the players seem to act dejected.

Vince Lombardi, the legendary head coach of the Green Bay Packers, said many memorable things. But this one is most pertinent to the Trojans and to the rest of us. Lombardi observed:

"Winning is a habit. Unfortunately, so is losing."

Expect to win when you deal with each and every prospect, and then you'll create the right habit pattern—one that befits a natural.

12. *It's never too late or a bad time to make money.* During the depths of the recession, I had an interesting conversation with a relative who happens to be quite a salesperson—at least when things are going well for him. When he has momentum, he's unstoppable.

Unfortunately, when he loses his keen edge his effectiveness plummets. When I caught up with him, he was reeling from a spate of bad economic news.

"Gary," he said wearily, "things are tough out there."

I'd never seen this sales champ so down in the mouth. He went on to tell me how past economic circumstances had been much more hospitable to making a buck.

I couldn't believe I was hearing a "Those were the good-old days" rap from this otherwise confident fellow. So, I decided to change the tide of our conversation, which like a whirlpool, was dragging me down emotionally.

"Look, Jay, times look bad right now, but I have news for you. There are millionaires being made at this very minute, and you're groaning about how impossible it is!"

He didn't expect such a broadside from me. Until then, I had been Mr. Congeniality, but I just refused to expose myself to his drivel. I simply wasn't going to buy that bunk.

Neither should you. If someone says, "It's too late" to earn sales or to make a good dollar, don't you believe it. Plenty of people are finding ways to get rich, if only by profiting from those who panic.

In bad times, there is a reshuffling of the economic deck. You don't have to accept the hand you're dealt or fold your cards and bow out of the game.

You can choose to run the tables with win after win. It's all a matter of feeling you DESERVE TO PROSPER. Yes, during recessions it can seem that everyone is suffering, and that it's somehow less than collegial to not bask in the misery as well.

But you don't have to, nor do your clients. A few months ago one of my consulting prospects gave me a typical stall when I suggested we get our training program underway.

"Gary, it's just a very busy time, right now," she pointed out.

I had heard that one before, so I offered this rebuttal:

"You know, Doris, there's NEVER A GOOD TIME to begin. You know you're always going to be growing and wearing a number of hats. So let's move forward, now, okay?"

She agreed, and later, when we were in the middle of our program, she said "Thanks for persisting with me, Gary."

13. *I'm the PERFECT AGE for EVERYTHING.* We live in a youth culture where images of vibrant young folks are paraded before us through magazines, TV, and movies. It is very tempting to start considering ourselves over the hill when we're nowhere close to an incline or decline.

Be inspired by the stories of people who just started to make it big when they surpassed certain ages. James Michener, the best-selling novelist, didn't write his first work until he was over forty.

Ray Kroc, the powerhouse behind the explosive expansion of McDonald's, didn't eat his first burger at the golden arches until his was well beyond fifty.

The age problem cuts both ways. Some very sharp people who happen to appear youthful can also be discriminated against. But there are ways to compensate for such adversarial circumstances.

When I was eighteen, I was attracted to teleselling as a vocation largely because I wanted my chronological age to take a back seat to my actual maturity level. I found that by using the telephone, only my voice was judged, and the fact that I was only eighteen and dealing with grownups didn't matter.

The same principle applies to using direct mail marketing. It is a blind medium in the sense that no one has to know what we look like, or even sound like, if we don't want to disclose that information. This medium makes it easy for people of any age to sell like natural born salespeople.

14. *I always get great pleasure from accomplishing what other people say I cannot do.* When I was a young athlete, I used to get a kick out of the fact that my adversaries from distant schools didn't know anything about me or my capabilities.

This meant that they'd position themselves in the outfield in all the wrong spots, thus enhancing the likelihood that I'd hit one over their heads, or at least somewhere outside of their running range. In other words, I relished the idea of being underestimated.

I still do. About a year ago, someone to whom I had delegated the task of making a sale for me said, in all certainty, that it can't be done the way I had proposed.

"You should do more research to find out what else is out there," she admonished. "Then, when buyers see you have done your homework, they'll express more interest."

I have a fairly refined "B.S. alarm," and it went off the second I heard these comments. What did I do? I took the project back, and I made it a point of pride to make the sale all by myself. And I'm sure you can guess what happened.

Yes, I sold this unsellable project in record time to just the right sort of buyer who my delegate said wouldn't respond to my persuasion. And what did I say to her afterwards?

I quoted Han Solo, the Star Wars character played by Harrison Ford. When the Princess expressed concern about the practicality of Solo's escape plan, he snapped:

"Never tell me the odds!"

Naturals feel this way about selling. Often they do things in an unorthodox manner, but they earn sales while their less gifted peers are left to gasp and wonder how they pulled it off.

Case in Point: Strong Language

I needed to get a fence-sitting consulting prospect to come down on the side of doing business with me, so I phoned him. Immediately after saying hello, I challenged him:

"When are you going to stop hemorrhaging money through your phone calls?"

It's a weird metaphor, but it worked. He committed to undertaking our project right away. Countless bean counters and apprehensive sellers would have urged me to make my language less bold and less graphic.

But what do they know? They can only recite the odds of success, but they've probably never beaten the odds in their lives!

15. *One courageous person makes a majority.* Groupthink drives me nuts.

When I was working my way through college I had to take a class in Group Dynamics. I hated every minute of it because the entire assumption underlying the course was that two or many more heads are better than one when it comes to decision making and taking action.

I wanted to cut to the chase and not waste time getting everybody involved in the decision-making process. Ready-fire-aim! That is my mantra.

I understand that P.D.M. (Participative Decision Making) makes corporate plebes feel warm and fuzzy, but for naturals it is a huge waste of time.

What does this antipathy toward groups mean to us as bigtime salespeople? A few things.

First, don't consent to do your selling to a committee if you can avoid it. Buyers who cluster in self-protective huddles are often a nightmare. I'd rather invest the time to meet separately with five individuals than to reap the false economies in dealing with a committee all at once.

To borrow an old expression, when you try to sell before groups it is all too easy to be nibbled to death by ten thousand ducks!

Identify the person who is first among equals and to court him or her. You'll definitely make more progress.

The same principle applies to dealing with people inside your own organization. The fewer you consult before striking out to generate sales or income, the better.

Case in Point: How Grandpa Revolutionized the Streetcar Business

My grandpa was a feisty immigrant whose first job was driving a streetcar on the streets of Chicago. One day he noticed that his coach was nearly empty at certain times.

Turning to his partner, he barked:

"There's no business here on 73rd Street. Let's take this thing over to 71st!"

Of course, his associate was stunned. Streetcars ran on assigned routes, and the entire concept of leaving your unpopulated route for a more promising one, was unthinkable.

Grandpa's partner went along with the idea, and for the better part of the day they were offering rides to entirely new faces. It broke the monotony, but it didn't go unnoticed.

As they pulled their vehicle into the terminal at the end of the shift dozens of managers and bigwigs were waiting for the runaway conductors. "Where were you?" they impatiently demanded.

"There was no business on 73rd, so we moved over to 71st. Look at how much more money we took in!" the excited drivers beamed. Sure enough, they had a record day financially.

The company did a few things as a result of the initiative the conductors demonstrated. They were reassigned to a busier route so they would stay out of trouble, and more streetcars were added to 71st Street. Oh, yes—they were also awarded a raise in pay!

Did That Story Tickle or Bother You?

If you laughed at this story and you admire the pluck of these two souls, you're probably well on your way to gleaning benefits from this book. After all, you identify with people who think iconoclastically, like naturals think.

However, if you read this tale with a stern frown while thinking that the characters were insubordinate and should have been severely punished, you need some help! You may want to examine your proclivity for siding with authority and the rule makers in our lives.

Yes, the errant conductors broke the rules, but that was the price they had to pay to try something new. As savvy corporate intrapreneurs will tell you:

It is usually easier to ask for forgiveness than for permission.

This means that you'll have an easier time ACTING FIRST and then seeking endorsement for your successful venture rather than hesitating to act while you're awaiting approvals that may be slow in coming, or that may be withheld altogether.

Sell first and explain later!

16. *I won't waste my time by judging my work.* Instead, I'll just do it!

If you follow this instruction, you'll build your self-esteem immeasurably while coming to feel you deserve to make sales. Whatever you do:

Don't become a self-critic.

Have you ever wondered why there have been so few player-coaches in baseball's major leagues? These are people who are good players, and they are simultaneously promoted to the level of acting as coaches or managers.

Strikingly few perform both roles concurrently for any lengthy period of time. How come? Because it's exceedingly tough to be a doer and a critic. You can't watch yourself run or swing a bat. At least not as effectively as someone whose main role is to do that.

By the same token, it is foolish to make the mistake of critiquing your selling performances. I realize this is a special temptation when you're sliding into selling slumps, and I'll show you how to conquer them, in Chapter 7.

For now, suffice it to say that you shouldn't get too detached or too intellectual about the sales process. If you do, you'll plague yourself with second-guessing about what you shoulda, coulda, and woulda done if you could buy your time back.

Don't bother with regrets.

17. *See every problem as a hidden opportunity.* During a recent slow period in my consulting business, I took a long and hard look at my overall operating plan. What I found was nothing less than stunning.

While I was building my practice, my financial investments were languishing for want of attention and careful analysis. I determined that I simply hadn't taken the time to critically evaluate my portfolio.

While millions of people were enjoying double-digit returns, my investments barely beat the money market. When I found extra time, I assessed my situation and resolved to improve it.

Within a period of ninety days, I executed a series of trades that brought my year-to-date return on assets to over 30 percent! I wouldn't have taken this step unless I had been forced by adverse circumstances.

I can't tell you how happy I am that I've hammered out an effective investment plan. In doing so, I actually have time to re-evaluate my business activities while calmly considering the best opportunities for growth.

This situation reminds me of the line Edward Albee wrote in his play *The Zoo Story*:

"Sometimes, it takes you a long distance out of your way to come back a short distance, correctly."

Problems promote effective side trips where you can generate breakthroughs that wouldn't have occurred to you if you had simply been humming along without a care in the world.

In the middle 1980s, I found it increasingly difficult to sell my one and two day seminars to colleges for sponsorship. Schools had been badly savaged by the recession, and they became exceedingly risk-averse.

At that time, I thought I was going to be in deep trouble because I had staked 80 percent of my marketing plan on working through colleges. Then I had an insight:

Why not shift my emphasis to offering in-company seminars and consulting projects?

This shifting of emphasis enabled me to transform myself from being a migrant speaker with no more than a few days booked at a given site to a person who signed on at companies to deliver, in some cases HUNDREDS of billable days at a shot.

Thus, the college problem turned out to have a silver lining because it made me improve my business model. I found clients who were interested in investing heavily into the six figures to improve their sales and customer service functions.

So a major problem helped me to give more value and derive much more value in return. Naturals make these adjustments all the time fueled, in part, by this feeling:

If I'm going to pay a big price to improve this situation, I'm going to definitely make it payoff, big time!

18. *I'm going to treat bad news as good news!* This may seem unrealistic to you, but what's the alternative? To get down in the mouth and then down on yourself?

Naturals are human, so they feel the sting of bad news just like everyone else. But they're tough enough, and smart enough, to transform a negative into something positive.

First, they don't confuse mere DELAYS or temporary SET-BACKS as permanent FAILURES. Like good sailors when the wind hits their craft head on, they make adjustments. They tack, or zig-zag their way forward so they keep making progress, albeit more slowly.

Seldom are they completely dead in the water unless they choose to be for the purpose of getting their bearings and setting a new course.

I'm a big believer in the idea that when the universe closes one door to us, several others are being opened at the same time. We can waste our time and energy knocking on the door that just slammed shut, or we can peacefully seek out the open doors.

It's up to us to decide how we're going to react to adversity. As the philosopher, Nietzche, said:

"Whatever doesn't kill me, makes me stronger."

Bad news is like a broken bone—painful to experience and somewhat time consuming to heal. When it does mend, it is often stronger than before it broke.

Like athletes, we can confront difficulty and elect to thrive on it. Keep telling yourself that this too, shall pass and it will. Something a whole lot better is probably waiting in the wings. I've found this to be the case when it comes to selling certain clients. The bad ones can actually push out the good if we aren't careful.

Case in Point: Finding Better Clients

I consented to do a needs assessment for an East Coast company. After meeting the owners, I determined that they were being less than completely honest with me, so, in effect, I fired them. I deliberately decided not to carry on a more extensive consulting program with them.

Life's too short for dishonesty and deception. The clients I terminated were shocked by my decision, and they couldn't believe that they were waving money at me and I refused to grab it.

I'm happy I didn't. If I had carried on with them, I wouldn't have been available to Transamerica, a much bigger and much better client that happened to come along the very next week!

I dispatched the bad news clients, and this made room for the good news clients. If you sense you're having a really tough time with prospects who are insisting upon receiving extraordinary concessions and unusual attention and treatment, you may be better off NOT SELLING THEM.

This situation is akin to intimate relationships. It's wise to remember this old saying:

A tumultuous courtship usually signals an even more tumultuous marriage to come!

19. *Remember the law of large numbers and always put it to work!* I learned about this law early in my selling career, and I'm happy I did. I've found that it applies to not only sales, but to many of life's matters.

What, exactly, is the law of large numbers?

Do enough of anything, and you'll get good at it. Do even more and it'll make you famous. Do more than anyone imagined possible, and you'll become a legend!

In selling, this applies to something as basic as telephone prospecting. The more times you dial the phone, the greater are your chances of speaking to someone who has the authority and the motivation to buy. The more presentations you make, the greater the odds are that you'll close someone. No matter what, if you keep on keepin' on, you'll probably make quantum leaps in effectiveness.

But what about pursuing quality? Isn't that better? Not necessarily.

Lots of us have been raised to believe that life constantly presents us with the same choice: either we can do a quantity of work, or we can do quality work. Supposedly, we can't do both.

This is a myth, especially when it comes to selling success. Quantity and quality are linked together for salespeople. In fact, the former usually leads to the latter, but the latter doesn't lead to the former. It leads directly to inactivity.

Here's what I mean. By doing a lot of work, of whatever quality, you'll inevitably produce some work of astonishing value. The odds are with you. Look at it as a baseball player views the batting cage. The more balls he swings at, the better off he is. His batting eye gets sharper. His swing more fluid. He remembers where his strike zone is, and he also gets repeated lessons in what happens, or doesn't happen, when he tries to swat at something too far from the plate.

It doesn't matter that the pitcher who throws batting practice is his old coach who couldn't get a fastball past a Little Leaguer in actual game conditions. The glory of batting cage work is that it isn't a real game. So relax and just keep swinging at balls.

The learning and ultimate achievement is in getting yourself to swing frequently and not trying to generate only one perfect swing. If you wait for the perfect pitch, you simply won't swing enough, and if you don't, you'll never develop a consistently high batting average.

Salespeople should try to be just as loose as ballplayers are in the batting cage. Even swinging and missing a lot of balls is valuable because it can alert the batter to the bad habits and traps he's falling into.

I mentioned earlier that quantity can lead to quality, but quality seldom leads to quantity.

I can make a pretty good hamburger because I had two good teachers: Fred Hayman, owner of Giorgio Beverly Hills, and the McDonald's Corporation.

Fred took me aside one day in his restaurant the Hamburger Tavern on Wilshire Boulevard. He wanted to show his chef how to make a classical burger, so he decided to prove his point by teaching an utter dummy to do it—me—his busboy.

Fred first spoke of how you must begin with choice or prime beef and grind it. Then, you make sure to give each patron a generous portion, and they are happy to pay a premium for it. Finally, the patty hits the grill, and your good judgment will tell you when it is finished to perfection.

Fred's approach was to go for quality. But alas, there aren't thousands of Hamburger Taverns around the world.

But there are legions of golden arches. McDonald's took a very different approach to teaching people how to grill burgers. It knew that quantity was the key to its business, so it operationalized exactly when to turn over a hamburger. (It's when little juicy bubbles form in the center of the patty and a discernible brown ring forms around the otherwise pink patty's edges.)

McDonald's' success is in replicating and improving upon the basics every day. But it never gets too smart or too elitist to stick with a winning mass market approach to food service.

Fred Hayman's genius is in creating value and a quality image, and that's why his Rodeo Drive boutique and his fragrances have flourished. But few of us, as salespeople, can do what he has done and succeed as well. For the great many of us who are in sales, the only assurance of a quality outcome and an above-average living is to be found in doing enough of the basics so we can't do anything other than succeed.

The hidden problem with insisting upon making perfect presentations to perfect prospects is the fact that we can spend so much time finding great prospects that we hardly ever speak to any of them. With fewer presentations we get out of practice; we get rusty.

Then it becomes easy to doubt ourselves because we haven't been in action for a long while. This leads to perfectionism, fear of failure, and procrastination, which means even fewer presentations and fewer chances of succeeding.

There's really no way around it. You need quantity to produce quality. As McDonald's' former chairman and mega-merchandiser

Ray Kroc put it when it comes to burgers or sales, we need to "grind it out" time and again to become successful.

20. *I'll continuously enlarge my sense of capability.* Naturals aren't afraid of bigness in any of its forms. They'll call upon and pitch the largest clients and try to close the most lucrative deals.

They feel they're worth it. The way they consistently generate this feeling is by enlarging their sense of capability.

Case in Point: Packaging Real Estate

Bill sells real estate in Glendale, California. He is reputed to be one of the biggest commercial brokers because he purposely keeps an expanding vision of the city in mind as he communicates with prospects.

This burgeoning sense of possibility makes him see opportunities where there are none. For instance, there was a small office building that came onto the market, and its listing expired. No one seemed to feel that he could make the property a valuable investment.

Bill approached the owner, but before signing him to a listing, he promised to do some research. He contacted neighboring land owners and asked them what price they needed to justify selling their parcels.

Everyone had a price! Some were higher than others, but Bill walked away from his conversations knowing that he could approach a large developer with a package deal. This would transform the expensive, little properties into a single, cost-justified investment.

Bill's a natural because he sees potential by continuously enlarging his sense of capability and possibility.

21. *I'll avoid griping and self-pity.* Complaining is an utter waste of time. Don't allow yourself to talk away your good by harping upon the bad.

Some folks delude themselves into thinking that participating in griping sessions is a harmless way to let off steam. I don't buy it. When you gripe about how a competitor took a sale away from you, all you're doing is adding to that competitor's psychological power over you. You're unwittingly setting yourself up for a repeat performance.

Watch out for the tendency to *blame others or circumstances for your errors or shortcomings.* Once you start blaming, you'll probably find there's no end to it.

By blaming, you "sell" your own power. In return, you "buy" a feeling of powerlessness from which it is difficult to emerge and succeed.

Case in Point: Selling Pity Is Better Than Buying It

I spent some time in the vacuum cleaner business when I was just seventeen. My sales training consisted of tagging along with a veteran who had been in the field for decades.

Frankly, I was embarrassed to be seen with him. His tattered sports jacket was dusted with dandruff, and his shoes had less shine on them than when they left the cow.

His instruction to me was to "Just zip your lip, and watch." It turned out to be a good tip.

We knocked on a door in a nice neighborhood, and a lovely lady answered it. He announced that he was canvassing the area simply to demonstrate the effectiveness of his vacuum, and he'd be delighted to clean her living room carpet for free.

She said okay, and the next thing I knew he was vigorously plowing the machine over the rug. He turned it off, and then he methodically opened the canister, removed the dirt bag, and proceeded to dump its contents in the middle of the lady's newly-cleaned carpet!

She gasped, which is exactly what he wanted her to do. Within minutes, she signed a contract to purchase this fabulous, state-of-the-art machine.

As it turns out, my mentor was the region's top salesperson, and when he was off-duty, he drove a new Lincoln Continental and dressed in neatly pressed, well-tailored suits, and professionally shined shoes.

His pitiful appearance before buyers was a show. He wanted them to feel sorry for him, and they did. It made them feel superior—

that they were doing him a favor. It also made them feel the vacuum wasn't packed with profit, which it was.

I share this story for a purpose. It's one thing to use pity and other emotions in your selling. They might serve a constructive purpose, and I'll dedicate a later chapter to the subject of exploiting the emotions to make sales. But it's a fatal mistake to pity yourself. That serves no constructive purpose at all. Like griping, the only place it leads is downward.

22. *I will always act enthusiastically, because enthusiasm conquers everything!* When I was in my first year of college, I had the opportunity to sign up for an advanced public speaking course with a gentleman by the name of Sheldon Hayden.

Mr. Hayden could have sold anything to anybody at any time. He was a true natural. When I took his class, he was semiretired and well into his seventies, but he emitted enough energy to run the power plant of a small town.

I not only studied with him, but I carefully studied HIM as he taught, and even as he walked to and from his silver-blue Cadillac—an unusually affluent car for a professor.

Every move he made seemed to be motivated by a serious purpose. He walked briskly, as if he had to share urgent news with his students and colleagues. And when this former Navy Captain began our sessions, he stood erect as if he were coming to attention. Then, he grinned broadly and carefully made eye contact with each and every one of us before uttering a word.

We knew we'd be changed by what he had to say, because even if it wasn't earthshaking in its own right, it would be delivered with thunder and unapologetic enthusiasm.

Mr. Hayden was one of Dale Carnegie's first contract instructors, and the course he had packaged for students was something he had delivered, by his own estimate, hundreds of times throughout the years.

Every moment of every session remained fresh and exciting, and that was this fine teacher's gift to those of us who were fortunate enough to get into his classes. It was the concept that, with enthusiasm, we can make everything come to life, no matter how dated some people say it is.

Hayden used to declare:

"Enthusiasm is the highest paid quality on earth!"

So, if you want to sell like a natural and build unshakable self-esteem in the process, be enthusiastic and you'll prove to yourself and to your buyers that you deserve to prosper.

In Chapter 2, I'll share with you the second identifiable trait of natural born salespeople. You'll learn how to create instant rapport and credibility with prospects by using humor, stories, and testimonials.

You'll also discover how to create the right atmosphere while fine-tuning buying moods.

CREATE
INSTANT
RAPPORT
AND
CREDIBILITY

Natural sales people use humor, stories, testimonials, and other techniques to create a productive and comfortable buying atmosphere. So should you. You can also learn to emulate the way they build their credibility by appealing to the rational requirements of buyers.

Why should people buy from us instead of from any number of competitors that we may have? We can hook them with a low price, such as a loss leader, but it's exceedingly difficult to retain customer loyalty based only upon discounts.

People initially buy from us based upon our credibility. They believe us when we assert that our products are the best or the most effective. But they stick with us in good times and bad for a different reason:

They stay with us, in large measure, because they like us.

Naturals appreciate that it's exceedingly hard to maintain customer loyalty while being despised.

Case in Point: The Cable Television Industry

For decades, many areas of the country couldn't receive decent television signals except through cable television service. This situation gave cable companies virtual monopolies over viewers who wanted a better picture.

The great majority of monopolies are not benevolent or kindhearted. They raise prices, almost at will, and they are notorious for providing a standard of service that ranges from indifferent to abysmal.

Cable providers infuriated millions of customers who eagerly awaited the chance to use an alternative. Satellite TV dishes have sprouted all over America, in large measure, because they represent the first viable cable alternative.

Now that they have competition, cable providers are touting service guarantees, installations by appointment, and other customer-friendly practices. But for many abused customers, it's too little, too late.

Naturals Invest in Relationships

Naturals realize, intuitively, that people buy for a number of reasons, but the main one is because naturals are enjoyable to buy from.

As a customer, if you are made to feel good and appreciated, and you sense you're getting what you want, you'll not only come back for more, but you'll recommend the experience to your friends and associates as well.

Naturals build relationships two ways: (1) they establish their credibility in such a way as to appeal to the left-brained, critical and analytical faculties of buyers; and (2) they arouse a sense of rapport and enjoyment by appealing to the right-brained, creative and intuitive meaning-centers of clients.

Unlike the Willie Lomans of the sales world who rely only upon building rapport and good will, naturals also appeal to the prospect's rational need to feel he's getting exactly what he's bargaining for.

Naturals know how to come across as people people. They're usually very effective communicators who put their prospects into a buying mood, but they also help buyers to justify their purchasing decisions. This chapter will reveal exactly how they do it, sale after sale.

Aristotle Was Right!

Over two thousand years ago, Aristotle boiled persuasion down to three ingredients: (1) Ethos, (2) Pathos, and (3) Logos. These terms signify: (1) the character, reputation, and good will of the salesperson; (2) the use of emotional appeals; and (3) the ability to make logical, rational arguments on behalf of the product or service.

We'll deal with using the emotions in a separate chapter. In this chapter, we're going to look at what naturals do to be credible persuaders by establishing 1) and 3)—their character, reputation, and good will, and we'll show the development of logical, "good reasons" for buying from them.

A Quick Lesson in How to Be Liked

Why do we really like certain people? As a general rule, it is because we see ourselves in them. In other words, we identify our interests or attitudes or backgrounds with them.

We perceive that we stand on common ground. We're linked together by our pasts, presents, or our futures. One of the keys to establishing rapport with prospects and being liked by them is to:

Be LIKE them.

You might think that's impossible if your skin color is one shade and theirs is another, if your sexes are different, or if you seem to have another stark difference that distinguishes you from each other. Gladly, this isn't the case.

We can overcome our differences if we establish enough apparent similarities, or if the similarities we establish are significant enough to us. There are several ways naturals do this.

Speak Their Language, Literally and Figuratively

Language is a miraculous tool for sharing ideas and information, but most of us don't use it well to create rapport and identification with customers. Naturals, however, seem to unconsciously exploit its potential.

Case in Point: Changing Impressions

My father was a natural who could charm people right away, even if he was speaking to them for the first time. When I was just a young kid, I'd observe him as he made cold calls from the house. What seemed utterly bizarre was his ability to shift gears when he spoke to different people. He'd actually alter his personality to suit his prospects.

In many cases, he drew upon his Midwestern roots to appeal to people who also came from that area. At other times, he adopted the smooth and melodious tones of a person from the South. And when he spoke to New Yorkers, he was quick and to the point!

When my brother, sister, and I would ask him about this voice changing, he'd just smile and shake his head as if he was oblivious to what he was doing. And I think he may have been unaware of it.

He just automatically adjusted his voice to appeal to the people with whom he was communicating.

By sounding like them, he seemed like them.

This resulted in a sense of identification, and people liked him and felt instantly comfortable with him because he sounded "down home."

Try Code Switching

If you don't already do this, you should definitely try it because it works.

What you'll be doing is switching your vocal code, or signature, to sound like the listener's. There are three comfortable ways to accomplish this:

1. change your rate (the speed of your speech);
2. change your pitch (the high and low tones you use);
3. change your volume (loudness).

You may think I'm asking you to sound artificial, but I'm not. I believe we all have multiple dimensions to our personalities, but we seldom put them to work. For instance, if you move from one part of the country to another, you'll start to blend into your surroundings.

Your language and tone patterns will gradually begin to sound like your neighbors'. I suppose you could try to resist this impulse to adapt, but it would be foolish.

After all, why continue to sound like an outsider? Don't you want to get along with your new peers? Of course you do.

When I found myself spending the better part of two years in Houston, I gradually started sounding like a Texan, even on weekends when I'd fly home to Los Angeles. My conversations were generously sprinkled with y'alls and howdys.

These changes gradually took hold of me, and I just went with the momentum. Once, when I had an extra day in the L.A. area, I took my car to a snooty dealership for repairs.

After the service technician wrote up the repair order, I innocently asked, "How long are y'all going to need the car?" He slowly looked up from his desk and asked, "Y'all?"

This demonstrates my point. I was speaking Texan in L.A., when I should have been speaking Californian. That is, if I really wanted to blend in and get along with the greatest number of people.

To sum up on code switching, you'll create more rapport and a better sense of identification with your prospects if you sound like them instead of unlike them. Listen up, tune in, and adapt to each individual. You'll be doing exactly what naturals do, and you'll sell more as a result.

Mirror the Prospect's Language

You're not limited to using tone in order to create credibility. You can also blend your text or word choices to the varied language preferences of prospects.

For example, say you're dealing with someone who uses action words that rely upon the sense of touch for their punch. He might say, "Let's rein this thing in, before it gets out of hand."

Or, he might say, "I'm trying to get a handle on what you're saying." It makes sense to respond to him with a mirror image of the language he uses.

You may decide to respond with some tactile words of your own, such as, "Here's how I grasped this idea. It could work for you, too."

When dealing with a buyer who uses visual references, naturals will automatically mirror them back:

Buyer: I'm trying to get a new perspective on this.

Seller: Try seeing it from this point of view.

We want to avoid speaking at cross-purposes. If the buyer said he wants "perspective," we're not going to offer him a handle to "grip." We're going to match his image to ours, even if we don't repeat the exact word he used.

When you adopt a buyer's images, you're speaking her language, and this is a speedy way to create a sense of trust and credibility.

Be Organized: It's Another Way to Be Credible

What's your image of a really, really capable person?

Do they seem to be engaged in deep thinking most of the time?

That's how I used to picture brainy, credible people. The great scientist, Albert Einstein, would come to mind.

Biographers have said that this lion of science was nearly run over several times, because he'd forget where he was and walk right into traffic.

Salespeople who want to appear credible to buyers shouldn't seem like they're in a fog. In fact, if there's one thing naturals do quite well, it is coming across to prospects as if they're in the here and now thinking crystal clear thoughts.

They do this by being organized in their thinking and speech. Being organized gives buyers the impression that they're in good hands, and that the salesperson is expert in his or her field.

Robert Maynard Hutchins, the former head of the University of Chicago, said it well. He noticed that true experts are people who don't necessarily know more than their peers. *They organize what they know, in superior ways.*

And what we know from everyday life and from behavioral research is the fact that *organized people are more credible, and credible people are more persuasive.*

It pays to be well organized, and this section will provide you with a great tool for doing just that. It's called the PEP format for persuasion.

PEP Will Energize Your Selling

PEP is a short-order formula for organizing your ideas. It can be highly planned out in advance of seeing a prospect. Or, you can use it improvisationally when you need to seem super sharp and crisp.

Here are the three components of PEP:

1. state a POINT;

2. state three reasons for believing the POINT to be true (EVIDENCE);

3. repeat your main POINT.

Case in Point: Using PEP to Answer Questions

I was called by a prospect in the employment agency business. After telling me he was shopping for sales training for his staff, he challenged me with this question:

"Of all the consultants in the world, why should I choose you?"

Here's how I met this challenge:

You should choose us for three reasons:

1. we have more experience than anyone else in the area;

2. we have tremendous references inside and outside of your industry;

3. we have the latest and best information to provide your people.

So, you should choose us, OKAY?"

This gentleman not only bought, but he did something else, which resold me on the great value of using PEP. When I began my training program, he introduced me to his partner while telling him how I had knocked his challenge "right out of the park."

Then, he repeated my PEP talk, nearly word for word!

What is it that makes PEP so effective? PEP is effective for three major reasons:

1. first, it starts with a clear, easily understood POINT;
2. next, it supports that POINT with three pieces of EVIDENCE;
3. finally, it reinforces the main POINT, by repeating it.

PEP is effective for three major reasons. That's why I say try it, and I'm sure it'll work for you, OKAY?

Obviously, I just gave you another example of a PEP talk. This time, I explained why it works so well. I'd like to point out a few more of its strengths to you.

- *You can use it to persuade or to inform. All you have to do is shift from telling someone what he should do to telling him about various items.*
- *This format works well in all media. Not only can you use it face to face and over the phone, but it is perfect for use in letters, faxes, and brochures.*

Let's spend a minute examining how it is most often used, improvisationally. That's how I used it with the employment agency fellow who threw me an unexpected curve.

What did I do, mentally, in quickly responding?

I transformed his question into a statement, and this provided me with my main POINT. He asked, "Why you?" and my POINT says, "Here's why..."

I knew that I'd have to support this claim that I deserved his business, so I said there were three reasons for believing my claim. Then, I commanded my brain to come up with them one at a time.

As each one popped into my mind, I simply packaged it:

1. we have more experience than anyone else in the area;
2. we have tremendous references, inside and outside of your industry;
3. we have the latest and best information to provide your people.

But I also Closed Him, Didn't I?

By itself the PEP format is persuasive, but naturals add a flourish to it, and this final touch brings in even more sales. They stick a close line onto the final point. You'll recall that I left my prospect with these words:

"So, you should choose us, OKAY?"

That final okay is exceedingly powerful. It's just the right amount of a nudge to get fence sitters to come down on the side of buying. People are conditioned to answer an "Okay?" with an "Okay!" aren't they?

I mean, you do it all the time, without even thinking, don't you?

I'm having some fun with you right now to prove the power of this form of closing. If you review the last two sentences, I ended each with a check back close, which is exactly what you're doing when you use an "Okay?"

It quite nicely urges someone to reflexively say "Yes," or "That's right," or "Okay!" right back to the seller. If you did that as you read my last few lines, then you've proven the point to yourself. Fair enough?

Gee, I can't stop these check backs, can I? Help me to stop, won't you? I think you're getting the point, aren't you?

So get organized, and you'll sell like a natural!

Why Do Naturals Use Jokes, Stories and Testimonials?

When I was in the car leasing business, my cubicle was right next to one of the funniest salespeople I have ever met. Alan should have been a comedian because he could do a million voices, scrunch his face into bizarre contortions, and just always make you wonder what was going to come sailing out of his mouth.

As it turned out, Alan got canned. Yes, he was way too funny. Management didn't appreciate the fact that the one impersonation he just couldn't seem to master was that of a salesperson getting a deal from a customer.

I mention Alan because he was anything BUT a natural born salesperson. He was really a joker, and his selling habits were a joke as well. Everybody loved him except the people who mattered—customers!

I'm not telling you this story to intimidate or force you into promising that you'll never again make a pun, cast out a one-liner, or enjoy a light moment. Actually, naturals use humor very, very effectively.

This section will tell you exactly how they do it so well without coming across as bozos or David Letterman wannabees.

Jokes and Stories Can Serve Different Purposes

Jokes can be used in many ways. If they're merely aimed at making prospects laugh, the seller could be attempting to break the ice and relax a buyer. They're also devices that humanize the salesperson in the eyes of prospects.

"Gee, Gary seems like a nice person," I might lead the listener to think. And, of course, why not do business with someone who is pleasant to deal with?

Jokes and other light references can shift the focus of a conversation that may be heading in an unproductive or negative direction. If you're about to discuss prices and costs, which can be inherently downbeat, a moment of levity beforehand could take the sting out of the situation.

I like to use stories to make a point that would be difficult to make any other way. When I use humor, I try to make it seem relevant to the situation so the prospect doesn't feel I'm simply wasting time.

Knocking Your Competition with Humor

You probably know that it's hard to slam your competition without having the attempt inadvertently boomerang and create sympathy for your foes. For example, if you knew your adversary's products were comparable to yours but their service was lacking, you'd be foolish to say:

Sure, they're shooting you a low price because their service sucks! We could low-ball you, too, if we never answered the phone!

I like to tell this little story, instead. It's called the Sanford Diamond, and it produces the same result without the negative fallout.

Mr. Prospect, I can only tell you what one of Acme's former customers told me. She said doing business with them reminded her of the story of the Sanford Diamond. June was admiring Edna's large engagement ring while saying it must have cost her fiancee a small fortune.

"Actually," Edna beamed, "It's the Sanford family diamond. It is beautiful, but there's also a curse that comes along with it."

"What's that?" her friend asked.

"Whoever wears it, also has to put up with Mr. Sanford!"

Sure, you get a low price, but what else do you have to put up with? This joke says, "All that glitters, isn't gold," but it sends the message in a fun way.

I really like to sell through stories because they amuse, and they also get prospects to see things from my point of view. And they accomplish this result in record time, with very little pain or embarrassment.

A buyer can laugh at the protagonists in a story and gently remind herself that it would be foolish to emulate their negative characteristics. But if we chastised her directly, and said, "You don't want to be a fool, do you?" we'd be shooed away in a second.

By telling the right sort of story, it makes you seem smart in a nonintimidating way. After gleaning the moral of the story, the listener comes to feel smart, as well. It is as if you have shared a secret, and now you're both better off for having done so.

As you can imagine, a tale like the Sanford Diamond can be used in various settings. Before you use jokes or stories, you'd be smart to check them out for hidden or unintended innuendoes that might hurt your sales effort.

Example 1: A Caterpillar Joke

I was told the following joke. What do you think of it?

What did the worm ask the caterpillar?

Gee, what did you have to do to get that fur coat?

I cleaned it up. It was a little less suited for polite company when I first heard it.

But I laughed, I have to admit. This joke bears some similarities to the Sanford Diamond, doesn't it? Edna gets a diamond ring, and the caterpillar gets a new "coat." But what compromises do these characters have to make to get these goodies?

Jokes are risky. First, your prospect may not get the meaning or understand the punch line despite the fact that it's perfectly obvious to you. Second, your buyer could be sensitive to the very material that makes the joke funny.

Example 2: **A Not-So-Funny Joke**
Roses are red, violets are blue,
I'm schizophrenic
And so am I!

If your prospect just happens to have a schizophrenic cousin, he may miss the humor in this. If mental health is a sensitive topic to the listener, you would be in big trouble with this one despite the fact that I think it's pretty clever.

What elements do the Sanford/caterpillar jokes have in common? In both cases the characters seem to be females. Some might say that they're females who are compromising their integrity or other personal assets to obtain material things.

To get a big diamond, which is the envy of her friend, Edna also has to put up with its donor, Sanford. And the caterpillar didn't get that snazzy coat for free, right?

Characterizing women, or anyone, in this manner is potentially offensive. Implicit in the jokes is the theme that the way people get goodies is by cutting corners or by compromising themselves.

You may think I'm making a big deal out of this, but one really needs to be careful with humor. What if we told the caterpillar joke to an animal rights advocate who believes the use of furs for clothing is disturbing and unnecessary?

My guess is that this person would get very turned off and would think we're insensitive as can be. Would women like these jokes as much as men do?

Originally, I heard the caterpillar joke from a woman. I'm not sure she's representative of her gender, so I don't know how many women would appreciate the humor.

One of My Favorite Sales Stories!

Here's one of my favorite sales stories. I hope you enjoy it!

A fellow in Alabama bought a railroad car of Florida oranges for $1,000, but before they arrived, he resold them to a person in Illinois, for $2,000. Just as they were pulling into the station, the Chicagoan sent them on their way to Oregon for the tidy sum of $3,000.

The Oregonian opened the freight car, peeled an orange, and was shocked to see that it had become rotten along its circuitous journey out West. He phoned the Chicagoan and lamented:

"These oranges are rotten!" To which the Chicagoan replied: "Those oranges aren't for eating—they're for selling!"

The punch line, "Those oranges aren't for eating—they're for selling," never fails to amuse people. From a humorous standpoint it represents a switch. Most of us see oranges the way the poor Oregonian sees them—as perishable food. But the seller has an entirely different agenda, doesn't he?

He just wants to sell them, no matter what. As you may have guessed, this story can also be used against the competition as a way of distinguishing yourself. If you want to assert that you're going to provide exceptional service and that your foes don't, you can say as much by telling this story.

All you have to do is apply the tag line to them:

And our competitors seem to believe that their air conditioners (or whatever the product is) are for selling, but not for servicing.

Try to develop a stable of stories that you can use to make your points. They're easy to listen to, people enjoy them, and we gladly take to heart the morals they convey.

If You Really Like to Tell Jokes

One more tip: If you really like to tell jokes, you should take a field trip to your local library. You'll undoubtedly find dozens of joke books, and don't be shy about stealing anyone's punch lines.

I sat next to a famous comedian on a plane and he told me that all professional comics have consulted joke books or had people write for them at various points in their careers. If it's good enough for them, it must be good enough for us, right?

Sprinkle Testimonials on Your Prospects

Selling is usually a subject that is viewed from the vendor's point of view. We concern ourselves with various techniques for persuading, overcoming, or avoiding resistance and so on.

An equally valid viewpoint is the customer's. What does this individual, or in a corporate setting, what does this group need to support the making of a BUYING DECISION?

Think of most buyers as just a little paranoid and you'll adopt an effective frame of mind for establishing your credibility with them. What do paranoids do?

They worry.

They ask themselves, "What if I blow it? What if I buy from this person and her widget is all wrong? Will I hate myself, or worse, will I get fired?"

There used to be an expression, which now seems a little antique in this fast moving, high tech world.

Nobody ever got fired for buying from I.B.M.

What did this mean? It meant that I.B.M. might not come through for you, but that would be unlikely. If you buy from the biggest and the best, then you've done the best you can do. And who's going to second-guess your decision?

If you buy from Schlumpo Computing, you're vulnerable.

How can a buyer make sure her decisions are bulletproof?

One way is by asking for references from potential vendors. If you're the vendor/salesperson, it's your job to make it easy for your prospect to buy.

Which is to say that you need to volunteer as many appropriate references as your buyer will need to comfortably and quickly award you with her business. To do this you'll need to put together a portfolio of great testimonials.

Get Your Testimonials in Writing

Having used testimonials for many years, I have a good sense as to what they need to contain in order to be really effective. The most critical thing to remember is to get your positive references in writing whenever you can.

To paraphrase a great Sam Goldwyn line about oral contracts, an oral testimonial may not "Be worth the paper it's written on." In other words, try get your clients to boast about you in a more permanent medium.

There are several reasons for doing it this way. First of all, your acquaintances in companies will come and go. They simply may not be around for you to have your current prospects call them.

And if they're already working for someone else, they're not going to be interested in recommending you on their new employer's time. Similarly, the entire company with which you've been dealing may disappear through bankruptcy or a merger.

Trying to get a reference in this situation is like trying to ferret out someone who has made a new life in a witness protection program. Good luck!

A more compelling reason for reducing to writing a customer's enthusiasm with you is the fact that memories fade and feelings change. Over time, your customers may sit on an emotional teeter totter when it comes to their opinions of you and your product.

If you're able to get a positive letter in one of their high cycles, this can be very helpful. This is the honeymoon period in a buyer-seller relationship when everybody seems happy. Take advantage of it and request your letter then.

Here's what you can say:

"Jim, how's our product working out for you? Then you're happy, right? Have I been helpful to you? That's great. Thank you.

"Would you do me a great favor? Could you just type out a one paragraph note saying that the product is everything it should be, and you've liked working with me? It would mean a lot to me! Thanks."

Am I twisting Jim's arm just a little? You bet I am!

I'm deputizing him to be my sales assistant, and his first duty is to bang out that nifty little note. Remember, this is our smooth sailing period, and if I'm going to receive a helpful pat on the back from my client, it's probably going to happen now or never.

But, you might be wondering, won't we receive some praise letters spontaneously? Certainly, but not nearly enough to help us to build a portfolio. We'll get 100 letters by asking directly for each one we get by simply waiting.

Once your reference is in writing it has the effect of casting your customer's opinion of you into stone. Imagine this scenario. You faxed Jim's nifty note to a new prospect who decides to get more details by phoning Jim directly.

Your new prospect says to Jim, "I see from the letter you wrote that you're very high on Gary Goodman!" It's going to be tough for your buddy, Jim, to eat his words if they're in writing, don't you think?

What can he say? "No, I lied in that letter!" Even if his attitude has changed, the letter serves as an anchor that will prevent his enthusiasm from waning in the future.

May I Quote You on That?

If you have difficulty getting letters, don't worry about it. You can still get testimonials.

You may have heard that word of mouth advertising is the best kind. It is—but there's only one problem. Satisfied customers don't tell enough people about you.

This presents a marketing challenge: How can we make our customers' satisfaction more widely known?

One of the best ways to do this is by obtaining an authorized quotation.

For instance, I was returning to a luncheon table during a break from one of my seminars when I overheard a participant praising my "New Telemarketing™" cassette tapes.

She exclaimed just as I was entering earshot, "Gary's tapes doubled our sales!" Instantly, I asked her:

"May I quote you on that?"

She said, "Sure." Immediately, I placed her fine testimonial into my national mailing piece. I also started mentioning her results when people would ask me about the program.

Your customers are probably praising you all the time, not only directly, but also to your associates. How many of these nuggets are being gathered and processed?

You don't have to wait for a quotable gem to jump into your hands. You can deliberately mine your customer base for them.

Exercise: Endorsement Mining

Call a number of recent buyers. Ask them what they think of the product. You'll often hear something right away that you can turn into a quote. Sometimes you may need to use a reflective question to put the polish on a quote.

For example, if you ask about your product's performance, a customer might say somewhat flatly, "It works." You can probe further. "Have you had experience with other products of its type that haven't worked?"

Then, you might hear, "Yeah, I've tried everything!"

The trick is to pull together into a single, dynamite quote what has been said in fragments.

"So, you've tried everything else, and this is the first widget to really work?"

"That's right."

"Great. May I quote you on that?"

Your quote will now appear this way:

It's the only widget I've found that really works!

There are hidden benefits to mining for quotes. By getting customers to praise your product you reinforce their original decision to buy while predisposing them toward buying more from you in the future.

You'll also hear customers telling you how they're actually using your product. It may be a surprise to you. This information can then enable you to reposition your item by advertising new benefits.

So, build your sales by multiplying the value of word of mouth advertising. Collect memorable and powerful quotations as a deliberate part of your testimonial gathering program.

Send Thank-You Notes to Your Buyers!

A good way to cultivate testimonial sources is by sending thank-you notes to your clients. If you show this form of appreciation toward them, you'll put them in a mood to reciprocate.

Some naturals keep track of their customers' birthdays and promotions. They make a special point of mailing them greeting cards and notes of congratulations.

Whatever you can do of a positive nature to keep your name in front of your customers is usually a good idea. Sending out calendars or pens with your name imprinted on them can generate good will and keep you uppermost in their minds.

In other words, the honeymoon may be over but courting your customers should never end. The testimonials they'll provide you may even grow in impact as they become seasoned.

Case in Point: The Growing Value of Testimonials

I designed and delivered a national training program for some very talented salespeople at Xerox. One of them left the company and went on to a great career with Merrill Lynch.

I renewed our friendship, and we have stayed in touch over the years. Now he is in management, and he is an even more credible testimonial source.

He says, "In all my years of selling, I've never found a better training program than Gary Goodman's."

And he has seen a lot of them!

In summary, natural salespeople use some clever techniques to create instant rapport and credibility with prospects. These include: (1) using vocal techniques; (2) using organizational tools like the PEP formula; (3) using humor and stories; and (4) using testimonials and authorized quotations.

In the next chapter you'll learn how sales naturals get customers to sell themselves!

CHAPTER 3

MAKE
CUSTOMERS
SELL
THEMSELVES!

Persuasion is much more effective when it comes from inside a person rather than imposed from outside. Natural born salespeople intuitively act on this basis. They get customers to sell themselves and so can you!

There is a sweet sound to success in selling. It's like the sharp cracking of a baseball bat telling the hitter that the ball is destined to soar over the fence.

This promising sales moment isn't the time prospects say yes and seal the deal—important as that is. It's when a customer lights up and says, "Gee, I could really use that!"

When the customer realizes and vocalizes his NEED for what we sell, we know that the closing of the sale will soon follow. Naturals are expert at getting prospects to realize and to articulate their needs.

Prospects Have to Want to Change

You may have heard the joke that starts with the question:
How many psychologists does it take to change a light bulb?
Answer: Only one—but the light bulb has to really want to change!

Of course, the idea is that psychologists don't cure people directly. They don't open people's brains and rearrange the furniture they find there.

They really help people to want to cure themselves. The same principle applies to selling, and natural born salespeople act, in certain respects, like savvy therapists.

They don't stand up and shout, "Here's your problem, Mr. Prospect!" They appreciate that observations shared this way would frequently be rejected. Instead, they ask questions to cause their clients to have INSIGHTS.

When insights occur, we arrive at certain realizations that encourage us to want to change our unproductive patterns. It's at that moment that buyers begin to buy.

Choosing to Buy Is Much More Agreeable than Being Sold

Naturals recognize that self-persuaded buyers are easier to close and more likely to stand by their buying decisions. They don't develop buyer's remorse and cancel orders nearly as frequently as folks who feel their arms were twisted before they signed on the dotted line.

Instead of behaving like the stereotypical carnival barker who hustles the identical snake oil to treat all ills, most naturals are surprisingly low-key who customize their persuasive efforts. This enables them to seem more like counselors or consultants than like self-serving wise guys.

One of the key capabilities of naturals is that they frequently don't seem like they're selling at all. Their customers feel they're choosing to buy instead of being sold.

Topflight Selling Is More about Listening than Talking

Being a glib, fast talker is not a good reason for someone to go into the field of selling, because the modern persuasion process doesn't really reward talkers. The big prizes are reserved for listeners who know how to interview prospects and draw out their wants and needs.

If we're speaking all the time, we're like dumb bombs that are fired in warfare. By foolishly aiming ourselves in the general direction of where we believe the target is we'll probably miss. Instead, we should be using pinpoint targeting that exploits the latest intelligence given to us by the targets themselves.

Why guess about the features and benefits that will turn on your prospects when they'll, generally, be more than happy to tell you precisely what matters to them and how to persuade them?

Suitable sales targets are people who express real needs and a current desire to fulfill them through our help.

Wants Versus Needs

I should distinguish wants from needs. Wants are satisfactions that we feel would be nice to experience. Needs are satisfactions that we feel we MUST have.

Can you guess which are more motivating to prospects? That's right, it's needs. Needs tell prospects: "Deal with me, NOW!" Simple wants, by comparison, can wait along with other niceties that remain on our never-to-get-to, wish lists.

Naturals motivate customers to transform mere wishes into urgently pressing needs.

Naturals Know It Can Be Smart to Play Dumb

Naturals aren't out to prove how smart they are. In fact, they respect that selling is an art where the art shouldn't show. If it seems to the prospect that we're talking too much while trying to actively persuade them, they can become defensive and erect barriers to thwart our efforts.

Communication theorists have noticed that the American population has become exceedingly hype resistant. American consumers have actually shifted from being passive to becoming what one observer calls obstinate.

Consumers now expect to use their increased education and critical abilities to get involved in buying decisions. If we don't encourage them to participate in their own persuasion, right from the get go, we'll be a lot worse off for it.

Naturals appreciate that it can pay off handsomely to dummy up and zip the old lip. Traditionally, sales manager have taught their troops to beware of over talking, and that SILENCE is frequently a more effective closing device than gabbing.

The smartest sellers know that they should restrict their comments through most stages of the sales process. They sense that if left alone in the presence of a reasonably reserved salesperson, most prospects will talk themselves into buying with very little prodding.

Case in Point: Letting Them Sell Themselves

When I was meeting with two airline executives, I put this non-blabbing principle to work. They knew that I taught salespeople effective appointment setting techniques, so after greeting them all I did was ask an easygoing question:

"Can you think of any people who could use telephone effectiveness training?"

I shut up, after this. In fact, I didn't have to say anything else for the next fifteen minutes except, "I see," and "Okay." My two prospects did all of my selling for me.

They replied, after smiling at each other, "Everybody, around here, could use telephone effectiveness training!" I knew at that moment that I'd simply be order taking after I briefly explained the mechanics of my program.

Naturals deliberately remove themselves as obstacles to buying. They get out of their own way, and the customer's, as well. They operate on the K.I.S.S. principle, which stands for Keep It Simple, Salesperson. (You may have heard this phrase as "Keep It Simple, Stupid!" but that's too derogatory, isn't it?)

I don't want to make the sales process appear to be overly simple, but you should know that selling shouldn't seem like a battle all the time. Occasionally, it is as easy as asking what I call a *perfect question* and then shutting up. That's what I did with my airline clients.

Next, I'm going to give you an explicit model for performing needs-based, naturalistic selling. I'll show you exactly how to get customers to sell themselves.

Anatomy of a Naturalistic, Needs-Based Sale

A natural's sale often follows these five steps:

1. opener
2. probing
3. discussion
4. focusing
5. commitment

Why does the sale move forward this way? It isn't because naturals find it inherently pleasing or always fun to do. Often, using this sequence compels sellers to be patient and to feel reactive instead of proactive. For vendors who need to dominate conversations there can be a sense of losing control over the conversation because the client may be doing most of the talking.

A natural's sale progresses through a five-step process because it is probably the surest and fastest path to the greatest number of sales.

I almost forgot to share the most important reason for this sales path. Customers truly like to buy this way. They want to feel as the conversation progresses that their wishes will be respected and that they're in the driver's seat.

As I describe this model to you, please perform a reality check on the validity of the information. Put on your buyer's hat.

Ask yourself, "Is this the way I like to buy?" I'll bet it is!

Let's begin this analysis of the anatomy of a naturalistic sale by examining openers.

Openers

A sale usually begins with an ice breaker, which I call the opener. Openers are attention getters. They provide you with a good reason for approaching the customer.

There are several effective openers:

1. *The Thank-you Opener*
This one is ideal for existing customers. They may have bought something recently or even long ago. This ice breaker

warms them up by showing appreciation for their patronage. The seller usually starts his phone call or meeting this way:

Ms. Smith, I just wanted to take a few minutes to thank you for your business and to tell you how important you are to us.

A thank-you shouldn't be reserved only for known buyers. It can also be extended to someone who read one of your company's advertisements and then sent in a business reply postcard to learn more about your services.

Mr. Jones, I'm calling to thank you for responding to our advertisement in Time Magazine. *We have a card here that says you'd like to receive more information about our new product line. To assure we get you the right information, I have just a quick question or two . . .*

Of all the openers, I like this one the most because it creates a positive atmosphere and it promotes the relationship between the buyer and seller. Just to show you how far a thank-you can be extended, let me demonstrate how I used it in a national sales campaign.

Case in Point: Fundraising

As a consultant I was asked to devise a program that would raise the average amount of pledges that fundraisers received. Of course, I did the obvious thing first. I instructed salespeople to double the amounts they initially asked from donors! (Once I convinced sellers that their more ambitious donation requests would work, we were on our way.)

That had a big impact, but we also faced a technical problem. We weren't working from a list of known donors to this worthy cause, so we couldn't tell before our calls were made who had given in the past and who hadn't.

The thank-you approach is very powerful when used with past donors because it makes them think, "I do give to that cause!" In realizing this, it cuts through the mental dickering as to "Should I, or shouldn't I give them something?"

They feel they should, and then the only issue to resolve is how much they should donate this year.

I'm sure you can appreciate how much I wanted to use the thank-you approach with everyone we called, and then it hit me! Why CAN'T I use it with everyone, providing I word it carefully?

I decided to shift from saying, "We're contacting you to thank you for supporting us in the past," to:

We're calling to thank you for all of the support you MAY HAVE given to us in the past . . . (PAUSE) . . . We appreciate it. (PAUSE) . . .

The results were nothing less than AMAZING. Approximately 80 percent of those we spoke to said, "You're welcome," after our first pause, and the remainder uttered a sheepish, "Okay," after the second pause.

In other words, listeners basked in the glory of having donated in the past, even if they hadn't. And this was especially helpful to sellers, because once prospects did this, they felt OBLIGATED TO DONATE THIS TIME to warrant the praise they had already accepted!

My recommendation: Use the thank-you approach generously. Remember, you can't go wrong by expressing your gratitude.

2. *The New Product/Service Opener*

Whenever you're introducing a new product or service, this is certainly a great rationale for getting prospects to pay attention to your sales message.

One of the tricks to making this an effective opener is to say your innovation is going to go a long way toward solving a customer's problems in a given area. Once that has been said, they'll open their ears for further details.

3. *The Demonstration Opener*

When you're using the demonstration opener you're promising to provide a taste of your product or service, generally for free. In demonstrating it to prospects, you're hoping they'll like it and will pay for more of the same.

Case in Point: Successful Door Openers

For example, a consultant or trainer might contact a company and say, "We're offering a needs assessment to help you to identify potential areas of improvement. This is normally compensated at our daily rate, but we'll be happy to do it free of charge to see if there's a basis for building a consulting relationship."

Let me reiterate that an opener is merely a foot in the door. If it gets the prospect's attention and has made the person receptive to communicating further, it has succeeded. It doesn't comprise the entire structure of the sales talk or phone conversation.

4. *The Inactive Account Opener*

This is used when we haven't communicated with a customer in a long time, or if they haven't purchased from us recently. For some unknown reason they've stopped buying, and we need to find out the reason.

The inactive account opener is a good way of reminding someone that we exist while discovering why they may not be doing business with us.

You can be very direct about unearthing any problems.

Hello, Mary? It's Gary Goodman, with Goodman Communications. (PAUSE) How've you been? Good. I was noticing that we haven't had the pleasure of shipping any products to you lately, and I wanted to see if there was anything wrong or if there's anything I can help you with.

This opener attempts to get the client to disclose problems, if there are any. After all, how can we fix something if we don't know it's broken?

To your surprise and delight, when you open your discussion with the inactive account method you'll probably find that most of these people aren't upset with you at all.

Case in Point: Opening Inactive Accounts

When I was doing a consulting project for a large paper distributor, we called on inactives who hadn't purchased supplies from the client for over a year.

We started the campaign with the inactive account opener, but after making a few dozen contacts we were pleasantly surprised to find that the great majority of inactives:

- didn't consider themselves as inactive accounts;

- didn't have negative feelings towards their vendor;
- were often ready, willing, and able to place new orders on the spot!

So we shifted to using the thank-you approach, which was more upbeat, and by making this shift we executed a very successful campaign.

My recommendation: If you're tempted to use the inactive account opener, start with the thank-you opener instead. Only if you run into a lot of grouchy people should you then consider shifting to the inactive account opener.

5. *The Special Sales Opener*

Nearly every company can use the special sales opener. Essentially, it offers a discount.

I nearly fell out of my chair when my jeweler used telemarketing to try to sell me a fairly expensive bracelet for my wife. Naturally, he mentioned how he was discounting it!

Of course, it's harder for dentists, doctors, and lawyers to pitch customers on a special sales basis. I can imagine that with some creativity professionals could extend special payment terms that would have the effect of extending discounts. They would need to accomplish this without cheapening the perceptions clients have of their credibility.

After all, if you're suffering from chest pains, are you really going to be attracted to someone who has a reputation as a DISCOUNT CARDIOLOGIST?

6. *Special Occasion Opener*

The jeweler not only called to tell me about the discount, but he knew it was our anniversary. (Talk about pressure!) Thus, he had combined two openers, the special sales approach and the special occasion approach, and that's perfectly smart to do.

Case in Point: Grand Openings

A client of mine in the air freight industry was celebrating the inauguration of a new terminal where it could unload several huge jets at the same time. So we formulated a presentation that invited clients and prospects to watch the action and take a tour.

Grand openings like this one occur all the time, and smart companies exploit them on several levels. They'll put out news releases in order to attract media attention. If successful in getting such exposure, the company will make the salespeople's jobs easier when they invite folks to participate. There will already be a wellspring of support for the event that sellers can draw upon.

7. *The Urgency Opener*

Naturals know that they usually need to arouse a sense of urgency in prospects to get them to BUY NOW!

One of the most frequently heard objections is "Not now. I'm going to wait." Buyers will stall unless they realize that they have a limited opportunity to get what they want at the price they want it.

If you look at advertising circulars, you'll notice that few things are sold without some sense of URGENCY. These words will appear: "Limit: 3 Per Customer," or "Sale Ends On Monday!"

You might walk or drive past a retailer's window where a makeshift sign reads: "We lost our lease!" This is a classical example of the urgency opener. It gets people's attention, and it says act now or you'll be sorry.

Case in Point: Creating a Sense of Urgency

When I used to travel a lot to perform consulting, I'd set up special week long tours. I'd earmark Monday and Friday for Chicago, and Tuesday, Wednesday, and Thursday, for working in Indiana.

I'd get on the phone and pitch prospects on buying one or more of the dates when I'd be in the vicinity. And I'd point out that they'd SAVE ON TRAVEL because I'd be spreading my costs among a number of sponsors.

This was a very powerful opener that focused the prospect upon a FLEETING OPPORTUNITY. Thus, they'd commit faster, and this would pare down my marketing costs. I'd end up spending most of my time doing paid consulting instead of in racking up costs while trying to sell consulting deals.

A word of caution: Urgency is perfectly reasonable and ethical to use, providing the advantage you're touting is indeed fleeting. You don't want to seem gimmicky, as if you're HUSTLING a person into making an imprudent snap decision. If you do this, your urgency opener will backfire, and create ill-will while potentially coming across as insincere.

8. *The Referral Opener*

The insurance business, among other fields, has been built upon a foundation of referral selling. Agents and brokers have taken great pains to ask prospects and clients for the names of three friends who might use my services.

This has solved a lot of problems. It turns what could be icy cold calls into warmer contacts. It also solves the list development problem, which makes every salesperson ask, "Who on earth am I going to call upon next?"

And it operates upon trust, one of the strongest of psychological bonds: "Well, if Ernie says you're okay—you're okay. Any friend of his is a friend of mine!" Doors that are shut to strangers are wide open to friends of friends.

All you need to do is initiate your communication with these words:

Our mutual friend, Bill Smith, asked me to call you.

If your prospect has high regard for Bill, he'll probably transfer Bill's halo to you.

But be prepared for the opposite reaction. Some referrals you contact won't feel that good about their old chums. I was given two referrals a while back to people who seemed to completely disrespect the referral source! Needless to say, I stopped using her referrals.

9. *The Affinity Opener*

A slightly different way to create instant receptivity is to build your approach upon a membership tie that you might have with a client.

This may have resulted from attending the same seminar or trade show.

Hello, Bob? It's Gary Goodman with Goodman Communications. I saw you at the recent Loyola seminar. What did you think of the program?

I'll get to the official reason for the call after I've broken the ice. This opener is really a subtle way of saying, "We have something in common."

When I was just starting my consulting practice, I noticed a brief article that trumpeted the achievement of a fellow graduate of the school where I earned my Ph.D. I felt an audience with him could give me some insights into starting my career on the right foot.

So, I phoned him and said:

"I'm calling to congratulate you on your achievement that was mentioned in the *Trojan Family*. I earned my Ph.D. at U.S.C. and I was hoping to have a brief visit with you when I get back to L.A." He graciously agreed to meet, and I learned a great deal from spending about forty-five minutes with him.

The old school tie surely helped to create immediate identification and a willingness to visit.

10. *The New Idea Opener*

Occasionally, you won't have an official reason for contacting a prospect, so this opener is really one that you make up as you go along.

Here's an example, which, if said with enthusiasm, will work as well as nearly any other approach:

Ms. Smith, I was reading the newspaper and suddenly I got an idea that I thought you'd be interested in.

Of course, you're free to invent opening strategies that are not mentioned on this list. Moreover, you can mix and match the ones I've provided to come up with hundreds of unique combinations.

For instance, you can use the affinity opener along with the special sales approach. You would be saying, "By being a member of the Auto Club, you're entitled to a 10 percent discount on your car insurance!"

Be creative. Remember that the opener represents your chance to put your best foot forward, so stride right. Spend time formulating this significant first part of your presentation.

The Credibility Statement

It makes a big impact to briefly state who you are and why you're worth paying attention to. I call this segment of the sale the credibility statement. It can be inserted just before you disclose your reason for calling or visiting.

Let's say I want to sell a top executive on one of my consulting or training programs. If I simply say, "I'm Gary Goodman, with Goodman Communications," the listener is bound to think, "So, what?"

But I'll get an entirely different reception if I say:

I'm Gary Goodman, with Goodman Communications. You may know me from my bestselling books You Can Sell Anything By Telephone! *and* Selling Skills For The Nonsalesperson. *The reason I'm calling is to follow up a letter I sent a few weeks ago. Do you recall seeing that by any chance? Gee, I'm sorry you missed it. I'll bring you up to date. It would have told you about...*

The fact that I'm a bestselling author is an attention getter. It says I've achieved a certain stature and I'm worth a little bit of this busy executive's attention. Without a credibility statement, I'm just another fellow from just another company.

Naturally, if your company has a certain claim to fame, this is the time to tout it. "We're the nation's experts in telephone training," might be a way to get this point across. Or, you can embellish it a little:

We're the nation's experts in telephone training, and our clients include companies such as Xerox, Polaroid, and a number of leading software firms.

How significant is the credibility statement? It's essential if you're selling upscale or high margin products or services.

Case in Point: Testing Credibility Statements

When I was refining a sales program for a financial company, we tried opening conversations with and without credibility statements. We found that we doubled our number of completed presentations after we included this critical step!

Probing

If we intend to do needs based selling, we have to uncover the prospect's needs as soon in the conversation as possible. After we have opened the conversation and have established our credibility, we ask questions geared to revealing unsatisfied needs, which our products and services can meet.

If we have probed successfully, our prospect will have three important realizations. She'll think:

1. I have a need.
2. It's important.
3. I want your help in satisfying it.

When your prospect thinks or says these three things, you have accomplished 80 percent of your selling mission. It pays handsomely to develop the probing tools to get these perceptions to occur like clockwork.

Here is the naturalistic sequence of probes that will get people to disclose their needs.

First, we should ask about their current circumstances. What are they buying now? How is it working out for them?

Second, we want to find out how their current purchases aren't serving them. What is the gap between what they want and what they currently have? This is the unmet needs step.

Third, we want to ask them about the importance of this need to them.

Fourth, we want to ask them if they would like our help in satisfying it.

So we probe for circumstances, unmet needs, importance of the needs, and their desire for our help. In doing so, we're using a motivated sequence for persuasion that is very comfortable.

Prospects appreciate it because it follows a comfortable, problem-to-solution pattern. There is a flowing quality to the questions. One seems to naturally follow another.

But you might be wondering, why bother with all of this probing if we already have a good idea as to what their needs are? There are no short cuts in a naturalistic sale, because even if you are right and you know all about a person's needs, telling them what their needs are won't make you as persuasive as you'll be when you get prospects to express them.

Case in Point: Learning to Listen

I was trying to put together a strategic partnership with an individual for the purpose of making a video program. Unfortunately, we developed some tremendous communication problems. When I would try to express my point of view, she'd interrupt me and declare:

You know what you need? It's this...

I can't tell you how much I resented these verbal intrusions. Had she simply listened and not tried to impose her ideas about what I needed, I would have been able to hear myself think and sound out my priorities.

I suppose that's what a needs based, naturalistic seller is: *a sounding board for the customer*. At least that's how it feels to be interacting with someone who knows how to communicate in the way most of us wish to be communicated with.

Let's take a closer look at the probing process.

Probing Example 1

A number of my consulting clients sell financial services and investments. One firm has identified affluent, older investors as their market. These individuals are drawn to investments that have low risk while offering an above average financial return. Typically, they put their money into interest paying accounts and Treasury Bills.

Because there is no urgency that drives these investors into the arms of brokers, sellers need to probe to develop a current motivation for prospects to change their investment allocations. A natural method of selling would have a broker introduce herself and her company, and then the conversation might go this way:

What kinds of investments are you attracted to, now?
I have my money in CDs, and Municipal Bonds, mostly.
Savings accounts, too?
Yes.
How are today's lower interest rates affecting the performance of these investments?
Well, I'm not getting what I used to get, I can tell you that!
How much less of a return are you seeing today versus six or seven years ago?
I used to see about 8 percent, and now I'm lucky to get 6 percent.
So your return has dropped by 25 percent or more?
I guess so.
Is that meaningful to you?
Sure.
How has it affected your lifestyle?
I can't see my grandchildren as often as I'd like.
If I could show you how to get a higher return on your investments, without sacrificing safety, would you like to explore it further?
Definitely. What do you have?

Naturals Engage Prospects in Lively Conversations

I'm sure you can feel how comfortably this conversation evolves. It sounds very relaxed doesn't it? Let's review what happened in this conversation:

1. We created some rapport and learned about the customer's current investment habits with a circumstances question. This tells the seller what he'll need to probe for to uncover needs.

2. We elicited an unmet need by asking how today's lower interest rates have affected the prospect. If a needs question is properly crafted, listeners will say things like "Ouch!", or "They're killing me!"

In other words, needs might burst through with great drama because customers are suddenly appreciating the GAP between what they've been earning and what they used to earn.

3. Next, we perform a very important clarity check to determine if the shortfall between what the investor once received and currently receives is meaningful.

There are probably some very wealthy people who couldn't care less that their return on investment has been cut by 25 percent. I don't personally know any of these folks, do you?

The key to this part of our probing is to get the prospect to say this is a difference that makes a difference to her. Once she says it's meaningful, she has unleashed an inner motivation to find a way to solve her problem.

By this point in the conversation she has heard herself say:

a. *My current investment practices aren't yielding what they used to yield;*

b. *Which means I'm losing money and the pleasure it can buy, and I'm concerned about it.*

All that's left to say is:

c. *Dear salesperson: Help me out*!

4. At this moment, the seller asks, "Would you like my help?" You can probably see how a well executed probing portion of a sales conversation can accomplish a tremendous amount of persuasion in a short amount of time. But before I continue, I'd like to address an important question that distinguishes naturalistic selling from other methods:

What if the prospect hasn't expressed an unmet need to this point in the conversation? In naturalistic selling, if the prospect doesn't say she has a need, that her need is important, or that she wishes our help in satisfying it, the conversation comes to a swift but gracious conclusion.

It's over.

No pressure. No haranguing. No pestering. Just a friendly good-bye.

Natural Born Salespeople Won't Force a Product or Service Upon an Unwilling Buyer. It's Not Only Unethical, It's Stupid!

There are plenty of prospects in the universe who have very real needs that they would love to have assistance in satisfying. In the same amount of time that it takes to hassle with a reluctant buyer, a salesperson can find two willing ones.

Naturals will also terminate conversations in this scenario:

He or she has uncovered an unmet need, but the customer doesn't think it's important enough to address.

Case in Point: Learning When to Walk Away

I performed a needs assessment for a personnel agency. After observing its salespeople, I determined they could really benefit from my training.

I reported this to the owner, but he said:

"Sure, they're not perfect, but I'm too busy taking wheelbarrows of money to the bank to train them right now!"

As a salesperson you can't fight this objection. You can try, but you'll be wasting your time. It reminds me of the saying:

Never try to teach a pig to sing. You won't succeed, and you'll only annoy the pig.

Here's another scenario in which you might think you have earned a sale but it is better to walk away:

You've uncovered an unmet need and the prospect says it's important, but she doesn't want your help in solving it.

As a consultant, I can tell you that I've run into plenty of prospects who sounded needy but who didn't really want anyone else's help. They want to bake the cake all by themselves. Small business owners who haven't mastered the art of delegation often act this way.

They may have called to get a bid or a proposal, but somewhere down the line they disclose that they just don't want to use an outsider for help.

When you utilize the formula I've provided here you'll learn this much sooner than you otherwise would, because you'll explicitly ask prospects if they'd like your help.

Please remember this. An unmet need that is acknowledged as being important doesn't make for a motivated prospect. They have to also say they want your assistance. Otherwise, kiss them good-bye!

Probing Example 2

The probing process is so critical to needs-based selling that I'm going to walk you through another example.

One of my clients sells a service to parents of seniors in high school. After announcing who they are and their company, the conversation goes like this:

> *Where is Mary thinking of attending college?*
> Loyola Marymount.
> *That's a fine school. Approximately how much do you think it's going to cost you each year?*
> I don't want to think about it.
> *I understand, but what's your rough guess?*
> About $20,000 per year.
> *Including room and board?*
> Nope. She's commuting!
> *That's quite a large investment to make, isn't it?*
> You can say that, again.
> *If we could show you some sources of loans, grants, and scholarships that Mary might qualify for, would that ease the burden a little?*
> It sure would. What do you have?

Let's review the probing sequence.

• • •

1. What was my circumstances question?
Where is Mary thinking of attending college?
It's a good question because it can elicit some friendly conversation while leading comfortably to the next step.

2. What was the unmet need question? You win if you said:
Approximately how much do you think that's going to cost each year?

A good way to identify an unmet need question is to see if it passes the OUCH test. If it gets a prospect to nearly yelp, it is a good one. Did this one pass the test? How about the one from the first example?

3. Our Significance question is:
That's quite a large investment to make, isn't it?
Again, this is a reality test. The seller of this service will inevitably find people who will say, "It is, but we've been saving for it from day one, so it's really to be expected." How should the seller respond?
Well, that's delightful. Have a great day. Good-bye!
That's right, it's a good time to pack up and to find someone who needs the financial help. There are plenty of them.

4. Our finale is the if-then question that probes for the prospect's desire for our help.
If we could show you some sources of loans, grants, and scholarships that Mary might qualify for, would that ease the burden a little?

How to Dramatically Improve Your Probing Skills

Your question asking ability and the quality of the responses you elicit will definitely improve with practice. To assist you in developing as fast as possible, I want to explain how you can put four powerful types of questions to work.

These are in descending order because we usually ask them in a top-down sequence.
Open
Narrow
Closed
Leading
We begin with open probes, advance to narrow ones, continue with closed questions, and finish with leading questions if they're required.

Each form of question is valuable in itself, because it will determine the amount and value of information that a prospect will give you.

When you put them together in the proper sequence, you'll find they can get the most tightlipped prospect to relax and give you any information you require. Let's examine each question in order.

Open Questions

Open questions cast a wide net in order to promote conversation. They enable a prospect to provide a wide range of answers. When we ask circumstances and unmet needs questions, they are usually open by design. Let's draw from the two examples above to see open questions in action.

What kinds of investments are you attracted to now?

Where is Mary thinking of attending college?

You may notice that these probes enable prospects to customize their answers to suit themselves.

Narrow Questions

Narrow questions call for a more specific answer. We used these narrow probes in our examples:

How are today's lower interest rates affecting the performance of these investments?

Approximately how much do you think that's going to cost you each year?

Both of these questions will elicit specific information that will help the seller. After asking them, you can expect to be provided dollar figures or their equivalents. Narrow questions enable buyers to quantify their own unmet needs. By getting into specifics at this stage of the conversation they're able to see the significance of their needs.

Closed Questions

Closed questions ask for a yes or a no. Here are a few that get prospects to say they want our help:

If I could show you some ways to get a higher return on your investments, without sacrificing safety, would you like to explore it further?

If we could show you some sources of loans, grants, and scholarships that Mary might qualify for, would that ease the burden a little?

If you want a very specific short answer, the closed question is the ideal type to use.

Leading Questions

As you might have guessed, the leading question is really a statement that is made in the form of a question.

That's quite a large investment to make, isn't it?

The leading question is the most intrusive. It almost forces a prospect to concede a point or to agree with the salesperson. I'm reluctant to use them, but if I'm dealing with a tightlipped prospect or with someone who doesn't want to commit to giving me information, I'll probably try at least one before packing up and moving along to the next buyer.

Probing The Reluctant Prospect

What if you are trying to sell to a shy person or to someone who isn't immediately forthcoming with answers that you can use to build your sales conversation? That's when you need to use the t funnel.

Imagine a funnel. At the top is an open question. A quarter of the way down the funnel is the narrow question. Another quarter of the way down is the closed question. Finally, at the bottom is the leading question. That's the t funnel, because it looks like the letter t.

I'm going to revisit Example 1, but this time I'm going to make the prospect much less communicative. Please observe what I do in employing a sequence of probes. I'll move right down the funnel to persuade the prospect to disclose an unmet need.

Example 1 Revisited

What kinds of investments are you attracted to now?
The same as I've always had.
What types are they? Savings, T-bills, bonds?
I have my money in CDs, and municipal bonds mostly.
Savings accounts, too?
Yes.
How are today's lower interest rates affecting the performance of those investments?
What do you mean?
Are you earning less interest on your investments today versus five or six years ago?
I might be.
What was the highest rate you were paid on a CD?
I got 15 percent once!
And now?
What am I getting now?
Right.
Now, I'm lucky to get 6 percent.
So your return has dropped by 65 percent or more?
If you say so.
Does that bother you?
Sure.
How has it affected your lifestyle?
What do you mean?
Are you having to be more careful with your spending because you aren't seeing those big interest rates?
I suppose so.
If I could show you some ways to get a higher return on your investments, without sacrificing safety, would you like to explore it further?
I'm listening. What rates are you paying?

I had fun writing this revised example because I tried to make it sound like some of my relatives! They're tough cookies.

When my open questions didn't work, what sorts of questions did I turn to?

I went down the funnel, sometimes in order.

For instance, the prospect balked when I asked her the circumstances question about her current investments, so I rephrased it into a narrow question. I gave her various options to select:

What types are they? Savings, T-bills, bonds?

My next open probe was about lower interest rates. This time my inquiry was rebuffed with a typical bounceback: "What do you mean?" I responded by using a closed probe to cut to the chase:

Are you earning less interest on your investments today versus five or six years ago?

If I had trouble extracting quality information at this point, I would have packed my briefcase, or, as a last ditch effort I could have used a leading question:

You can't be as happy now with today's puny interest rates when compared to the higher rates of years gone by, RIGHT?

If a leading question doesn't hit the mark, call the Coroner because your prospect doesn't have a pulse!

At times you may feel you're being called upon to spoon-feed questions to your prospects. Be patient with them. It could be that they're not used to communicating in detail about what you're trying to sell.

You may recall that I had to convert a narrow question into a closed type and ask the same basic question a few different ways to get a useful answer:

How has it affected your lifestyle?

What do you mean?

Are you having to be more careful with your spending because you aren't seeing those big interest rates?

Some Final Words on Probing

I hope you'll see that Probing is critical to the way natural born salespeople work. Although it may appear a bit mechanical to you right now because we're slicing and dicing it so many ways, sales naturals do it almost without thinking. It works very, very well.

It definitely gets the customer to open up and deliver quality information to you, the seller. It gets them to say that (1) they have a need; (2) it's important; and (3) they want your help to solve it.

Once these words escape their lips, they have more or less sold themselves. Usually, at this point of the conversation they'll start closing the sale by themselves. Realizing their needs, they'll ask: *What do you have for me?*
At that moment you're not selling. They're buying!

Now that you understand how to probe, we need to master the remaining steps truly natural salespeople use to make sales. These include the discussion, focusing, and commitment steps.

The Discussion

The Discussion segment of the natural's sale is fairly straightforward. Its purpose is to provide the customer with various options for solving her problems.

In the investment example, the seller could have followed his probing with a description of two or three of the investments with which she is familiar that could provide an above average return with low risk.

In our college financing example, the sales rep could have discussed a few sources of loans or grants that might be available, yet still unknown to the parent.

Offer a Menu of Buying Options in Your Description

Needs-based selling tries to offer more than one solution whenever possible. This gives the buyer the comfort of knowing she has choices that can help her to address her unmet needs.

It also helps the seller to avoid seeming like a person who is pitching one solution to fit everyone's needs. If you fall into that trap, you can lose a lot of credibility.

Once you have discussed various potential solutions, you can introduce a step that is very specific to the way naturals sell. It is the focusing step.

Focusing

When we have discussed potential solutions, it is very appropriate to ask the prospect:

At this point, which of these options would you like to pursue further?

This puts the buyer into the driver's seat. It's his job to tell you what is attractive to him and what isn't. If there is a solution that he simply doesn't want to pursue, he'll probably steer you away from it. This is great because it will save you time, and you'll save face and potential embarrassment by not committing the prospect to a potential solution that he isn't interested in.

Once your buyer has focused upon what's attractive, all you need to do is flow through to the commitment step of the conversation.

Commitment

Engineering commitment is essential to effective selling.

Naturals don't sweat this part of the sale because they do it the easy way. Instead of trying to close the sale from the moment she's in the prospect's presence, the natural will allow the close, or what I'm referring to as commitment, to organically emerge from the steps that preceded it in the exchange.

In other words, making a commitment shouldn't seem like a major step for the buyer to take, and if you perform it right, more often than not the buyer will close himself before you ask him for the order!

Case in Point: Selling Software Upgrades

One of my clients manufactures a software product that increases the memory that a user can access on his or her personal computer. Unlike hard memory, which involves opening up the PC and inserting more RAM, a software fix is as easy as popping a floppy disk into the machine and clicking the mouse a few times.

Getting memory this way is usually cheaper because you don't have to pay a technician. You can easily do it yourself. My client wanted to phone existing users and offer them an upgrade at a very reasonable price. There was only one slight problem. Happy customers would be more than likely to offer the objection that they currently had enough memory.

As you know, if there's no need, there's probably no sale! So I designed a needs-based sales plan that emulated the anatomy of a naturalistic sale that I've presented in this chapter.

The following is the text of an actual call where the customer sold himself. Our probes were designed so that prospects would arouse in themselves a strong perceived need for the upgraded product. (Only the names have been changed in this transcript.) The representative's part is italicized.

Hello, Mr. Lee?

Yes, who's this?

It's Jill, from Quality Software Associates, on a recorded line. How are you this afternoon?

Okay, I guess.

Well, good. I'm calling to thank you for using our ABCD Software.

Oh, you're welcome.

And we also wanted to see how it's working for you.

It's working great.

That's good. What other applications are you running?

Oh, a little of everything—spreadsheet, word processing, you know.

And do you normally upgrade those when new versions come out?

Yes.

How can we make our software more effective?

Well, give me more memory!

Well, you can always use more memory, can't you?

Yes, that's right.

Well, that's why we've come out with ABCD Version Six. It gives you up to 25 percent more memory, and it's compatible with all your other applications, and it only runs $30 to upgrade. So...

(Interrupting her) Well, send it out!

Okay, we'll get a copy out to you and we know you'll be pleased, okay?

Yes, fine.

All I need is a major charge card number.

If you take a close look at this transcript you'll notice several important ingredients that we've covered in this chapter. First, what kind of opener does Jill use?

That's right, it's the thank-you opener. It really warms people up. In this call, the customer was actually a little defensive in the beginning. Recall that he asked, "Who's this?" very suspiciously. When Jill told him and thanked him for his business, he brightened immediately.

What kind of question did she start with as she entered the probing segment? If you said a circumstances question, you're right on the money. She asked how her software was working for him.

This is a great question to ask an existing customer because it gets him to RESELL HIMSELF ON THE WISDOM OF HIS ORIGINAL PURCHASE. Think about that for a second.

As a seller, don't you want your clients to refresh themselves about how great your products are before you move forward to sell another one? It just makes good sense to ask.

Jill then asks her first unmet needs question:

What other applications are you running?

Here's the background you need to know to appreciate the importance of this apparently casual probe.

First, you should know that the software biz is a lot like the boom days in the car industry. Remember those fins on Caddies and other road boats? Engines got bigger and bigger and fuel efficiency grew worse and worse.

Software has been the same way, but instead of guzzling gas, new applications guzzle memory because they come loaded with a lot of bells and whistles that most people don't use.

By finding out about the other applications, Jill was getting the prospect to appreciate, subliminally, that he needs memory to access them. The next question seals this proposition:

Do you normally upgrade them when new versions come out?

This is aimed at getting the buyer to appreciate that he's in the habit of upgrading, so when he discovers there is a new version of ABCD to which he hasn't upgraded he'll want to remedy this oversight.

Then the clinching question is asked, which gets prospects to sell themselves:

"How can we make our software more effective?"

I designed this sales interview so clients would say exactly what Mr. Lee said:

"Well, give me more memory."

Not only is he saying that he needs memory and is ready, willing, and able to buy it if you have it, he's doing something else that's incredibly meaningful. He's overcoming the most devastating objection he could raise.

You'll notice that Jill reinforced him after he said these words. She replied before moving into the discussion portion of her sale with:

"Well, you can always use more memory, can't you?"

I inserted this line into the presentation if prospects failed to volunteer, "Give me more memory." If she had asked how can we make ABCD more effective, and Lee said, "Beats the heck out of me!" she could have instantly elicited the need by asking the leading question:

"Well, you can always use more memory, can't you?"

We're covered no matter how a customer responds. I hope you'll see from this example how naturals seem to sell effortlessly. It's a wonderful process because the customers do persuade themselves, and as you can see from the example, Mr. Lee actually took the close away from Jill when he interrupted her and said:

"Well, send it out!"

If you're used to a mechanical spray-and-pray approach to selling, you're probably shaking your head and thinking, "No, way! Buyers just don't close themselves."

Ah, but they do it all the time for naturals.

Let's Talk about Objections

No sales book would be complete without information dealing with the answering of objections. An objection can be defined simply as *a prospect's reason not to buy what you are selling.*

Salespeople hear them all the time. But I can tell you this: Naturals hear fewer objections than their peers, and they decide to answer only a small percentage of those they do hear!

What do I mean? Aren't salespeople supposed to rhetorically slug it out with reluctant prospects? Traditional sales training says

"Yes! Defeat these wormy, negative intrusions that prospects insinuate into your otherwise smooth presentations. Wear them down!" In fact:

Never take no for an answer! Never! Never! Never!

Well, as you can imagine, having read this book to this point, we're going to break with tradition. Yes, I'll teach you how to do battle with customers, but I'd prefer to show you how to avoid spats altogether.

You'll Hear Very Few Objections with Needs-Based Selling

Let's do a quick review. It is a natural's job to use the first part of a sales interview to elicit from the prospect three statements: (1) I have a need; (2) it's important; and (3) I want your help.

Imagine this scene. You've gotten a prospect to say these three things. You're about to recommend a few options for satisfying his needs. How likely is it at this advanced stage of your relationship that he'll try to shoot down your conversation with a typical objection?

I can tell you that it's extremely unlikely!

You'll definitely find people who won't express a need for your product or service, but that isn't the same as objecting to your sales effort.

If you're in the unmet needs stage, you haven't even gotten to the point where you're offering prospects a specific item for their consideration.

So what can they object to?

If there is no need, what do you do? You don't square off with them and argue about the idea that they SHOULD HAVE A NEED! You say good-bye, and move on to the next person.

Case in Point: Learning When to Walk Away 2

A smiling face knocks at your door and says, "Hi, I'm with the Daily News and I'd like to introduce myself...." You reply, "Well, thanks anyway. I subscribe to the *Times*. Bye!"

What's a seller to do, simply walk away? Yes, he could do that, but he'd run the risk of seeming like a wimp to his manager while feeling that his prospects are besting him.

So he learns a technique for rebutting objections, then he rhetorically slugs it out with homeowners. As a buyer, do you really want to fight with a news vendor at your front door, or anywhere for that matter?

Okay, You Twisted My Arm—I'll Teach You How to Answer Objections

I do think it's important to give you a solid technique for managing objections because they can't all be avoided, and you may as well be prepared with a full complement of tools at your disposal.

There are six frequently heard objections:

1. No money
2. No value
3. No interest
4. No need
5. No time
6. No authority to buy

Let's say the customer uses objection (1), and she says, "I can't afford it." There is a pat formula for addressing this assertion and other objections. You can respond with:

Well, I appreciate that, but this will pay for itself within one year. So give it a try, and I know you'll be pleased, okay?

There are three parts to this response.

1. *The Transition Phrase.* It agrees, temporarily, with the buyer. It is necessary to take the sting out of the direct contradiction that follows. In this example the transition phrase was:

Well, I understand that, but . . .

2. *The Rebuttal.* This is the actual contradiction. It says, nicely, of course, "I disagree!" In this example the rebuttal was:

. . . this will pay for itself within one year.

3. *The Clutch Close*. This is a way of securing instant, almost knee-jerk, approval.
So, give it a try, and I know you'll be pleased, Okay?

What is a prospect saying when she asserts she has no money? That she's utterly broke with no ability to make discretionary purchases? This is possible, so you should ask yourself if it is even worth countering her claim.

Might you be better off to believe her and to move on to the next, and we hope, more solvent prospect? The same logic applies to the no interest objection. Why not simply BELIEVE a prospect who says this instead of continuing our spiel in the hope that, sooner or later, we'll luck into uttering something in which she'll be interested?

Generally, when you perform naturalistic selling you'll hear "I'm not interested" only at the very beginning of the conversation. It's almost a reflexive and self-protective reaction prospects have who fear that we're going to waste their time or suck out every last drop of their life force.

Actually, there is a way of getting them to listen to about two or three more lines after they've said "Not interested." If you're very quick on the up take, you can bridge back to your talk with this phrase:
Well, I'd be surprised if you were at this point, but . . .

I know that, this line looks terrible on the page, doesn't it? But if you deliver it in a friendly, low-key tone of voice, it'll actually be received pretty well. How come?

Think about it for a second. What are we REALLY saying here? We're saying, "Look, if I walked up to you, and right after I announced my company's name you replied, 'GEE, I'M INTERESTED!' Well, I'd be more than a little surprised."

So it's a logical line.

Example: Answering Lack of Interest
Here's how it works in context:

Hello, I'm Gary Goodman with Goodman Communications . . .
I'm not interested.

Well, I'd be surprised if you were at this point, but I'm follow-ing up a mailer I sent out. Do you recall seeing it by any chance?

By this point in the conversation the prospect will be thinking about the content of my question and not about the transition phrase I used on him.

What's the best way to get someone interested in something? By probing for his needs, that's how. So, again, if you do an effec-tive job of bringing out a person's motivation, you won't have much demand for answering objections of the not interested type.

If someone is saying "It's too expensive," or it "Costs too much," she's really saying you haven't established your product's value. When you have gotten a prospect to say she has a need and it's important enough to address, you'll hear the no value objection very infrequently.

Example: Answering Price Objections

I do a lot of my own investment trading over the Internet at an exceedingly low commission rate. I also trade through a broker, but his commissions are outrageously high by comparison.

What if he came to me and he asked what my overall return was in my self-managed portfolio, and I replied 15 percent per year. If he said he has averaged over 25 percent for clients AFTER HIS COMMISSIONS HAVE BEEN PAID, I'd hear a very good answer to my objection that his commissions are excessive!

When customers are complaining about price, they're really telling us to ratchet up our value, and to do it fast.

When a prospect says she doesn't have time to talk, I have a very quick and simple reply:

"Well, I appreciate that and I'll make it brief."

What's her worst fear, the one that's lurking behind her objec-tion? It's that I'll talk her ear off. So I assure her I won't, and I con-tinue with the interview as if the interruption had never occurred.

If someone says they have no authority to buy, believe them and ask to be put in touch with the decision maker. Just today I got an e-mail from someone who said, "My boss is in Canada, and I'd like you to send him some information."

Is he kidding? When the boss makes the literature request, I'll probably respond, but not to someone without authority. (This objection also gets us onto the topic of never wasting your time, which we'll discuss a later chapter.)

Suffice it to say that you can answer every objection if you want to. Make sure that it's worth your effort to do so instead of moving on to communicate with the next, potentially objection-free, client.

You've seen exactly how natural born salespeople get prospects to sell themselves. In the next chapter you'll learn another exciting secret of naturals: how they harness the power of the emotions to do their selling.

CHAPTER 4

PUT
THE POWER
OF EMOTIONS
TO WORK

Selling manuals often miss the HUGE role that the emotions play in buying behavior. When folks WANT TO BUY or DON'T WANT TO BUY. This transcends many other interests they have. Let's look at how natural born salespeople use these emotions to sell better and faster.

Yogi Berra had the right idea when he noticed, "If people don't want to come to the ballpark, then nothing can make them come to the ballpark."

Berra meant that people won't do what they don't WANT to do. This seems terribly obvious, but most salespeople, sales managers, and sales trainers overlook this fundamental fact.

Too often, sales professionals approach the sales process as if it were a matter of stiffly establishing the seller's credentials or clinically providing features and benefits to get prospects to say yes. These elements certainly can inform buying decisions, but they're vastly overvalued.

Case in Point: Poor Service

There is a restaurant that has good food at low prices, but their service stinks. Recently, my daughter stained a new outfit by sitting in one of their unwiped booths.

"What do you want US to do?" the manager challenged after we informed him of his restaurant's sloppiness.

Rather than hassle with them to persuade them to pay for dry cleaning, we scrubbed out the stain. As I write these words, I can honestly say we're deliberately staying away from this restaurant.

We're punishing them. In other words, WE DON'T WANT TO BUY FROM THEM.

This is a lose-lose conflict because we're missing their food, and I presume they're missing our money. But we won't go back because we want them to PAY for their foolishness and for their cavalier approach to customer satisfaction.

To paraphrase Yogi, nothing can make us buy if we don't want to buy. I see this all the time in my own behavior as a consumer, especially when I walk into department stores with members of my family. They might be eager to try on clothes, while I can't wait to escape.

Everything might be ON SALE. In fact, they could be giving their goods away, but I still may be in no mood to buy. I'm sure you can relate to this feeling, right?

The converse applies as well. Sometimes I'm in a great mood to spend. When I'm on vacation, I'll pull out most of the stops. I order exactly what I want in restaurants, and if I discover that I forgot to pack my swim suit, I'll plunk down whatever it takes to replace it with little regard to the price tag.

I bought my house this way. I had admired it for a long time, and then, suddenly, it had a for sale sign in the lawn. I called my realtor, did a quick walk though, and started negotiating. It was, and is, one of the most satisfying purchases I've ever made.

I WANTED it, and that made all of the difference. Sure, I could have been hyper rational in my approach to the process, but that's not much fun and it's also a lot of hard work. Buying something should be enjoyable, don't you agree?

Sellers who know how to set the right mood and to exploit emotions properly are rewarded handsomely for their efforts. But they are few and far between.

Most salespeople spend far too much time with details that real, motivated, and impassioned buyers have little patience for or interest in. For example, I took a test drive of an all-purpose vehicle the other day. All I wanted to do was FEEL how it drove. If it FELT GREAT I was going to increase my interest in buying it. And if I didn't find pleasure in the grip of the steering wheel, or in the way it cornered, or in its acceleration, I wasn't going any further in my research.

The salesman wasted a ton of time previewing the car for me. He showed me the engine, which is like playing a beautiful sonata for someone who has his hearing aid turned off. He showed me the cargo hold and boldly asked me if I had ever seen such cubic footage. In all honesty, I had to reply that I had more space in my current station wagon.

Finally, we got in and I drove it. I'm fairly tall, and my left leg couldn't completely extend, which makes me nuts when I rent cars for business. At that point, I told him I simply couldn't consider the car any further.

All of his silly verbiage about presumed features and benefits was wasted, and I actually resented going through the drill. I felt he wasted my time with needless preliminaries, and I could tell he was dejected because I unceremoniously terminated my interest in the vehicle.

If he had appreciated the fact that I don't buy features and benefits in cars—I buy the FEELING of them—we could have cut to the chase and saved a half-hour. His rapping about the slant-six engine and the tinted glass meant absolutely nothing to me.

Am I saying there is no place for features and benefits in selling? No, they can play a role, but that role should be relegated to reinforcing a WANT. If the WANT hasn't been aroused, sellers can forget about going any further.

A natural would have sized me up within seconds. He would have sensed that I'm a driven type of personality (no pun intended). And he would have backed off while allowing me to conduct the sale to meet my needs.

He might have asked, "Is there anything special you're looking for in an S.U.V.?" That would have given me the chance to have said, "Yeah. I want it to feel tight, especially around corners. And I don't want to feel like it's going to tip over."

That would have communicated to the sales rep, "Get this guy behind the wheel A.S.A.P.! If he likes the way it drives, you've got a sale."

Buying Requires Right-Brain Excitement and Left-Brain Justification

If I had loved the feeling of the car, and I got serious about buying it, I might have been able to use some left-brain, linear, rational reasons for doing so. Then, hearing about its great warranty and antirust undercoating might have helped me to JUSTIFY DOING WHAT I HAD ALREADY STARTED DECIDING I WANTED TO DO.

Let me make a clear point that left-brained, good reasons for buying are secondary for most folks. People buy faster, buy more, and feel better about their purchases when we encourage them to use their right-brain in the process.

The right hemispheres of our brains are responsible for many of our intuitive, artistic, and impulsive reactions. Sizes, shapes, and global, big picture phenomena are processed there. It wouldn't be quite accurate to call this part of our consciousness irrational, but it does seem to operate differently than left-brain reasoning processes that are reducible to logic.

Natural born salespeople appreciate the fact that most people don't bring out spreadsheets when they start buying things, large or small. I haven't seen any customer use Ben Franklin's suggestion to make two columns, count the entries pro and con, and then decide to choose the more reasoned and weighty course of action or inaction.

They generally say to themselves, I LIKE THIS! Or, they listen to a salesperson and say, I LIKE HER! It's akin to seeing a great painting or hearing a wonderful tune that suddenly delights you. You don't know WHY you're enchanted by it, but you like your reaction and you're willing to go with it. (Unless a left-brained salesperson confuses you with the facts and scares you away or turns you off.)

You might enter a restaurant for the first time and instantly feel at ease. You haven't ordered yet, but this doesn't stop you from appreciating where you are because the environment is doing something to you. It's arousing your appetite. You're not going to just stick to ordering a soda, you're going whole hog!

May I See the Wine List, Please!

What transformed you from being a frugal, careful diner, into a carefree spender? This is what natural born salespeople bring about in us. We're going to explore how they arouse the PASSIONS of buyers, to make us want to buy, and most important, to make us want to buy FROM THEM RIGHT NOW.

If you're an experienced seller, does this mean you'll need to abandon everything you have learned about selling just to follow the methods outlined here?

If you're already a natural born salesperson, the chances are strong that you're already intuitively using some of these techniques. Your more organic, freely flowing approach to selling is probably an exceedingly comfortable one for buyers to relate to.

How Putting Emotions to Work Put Me to Work

When I had just finished high school, I looked for a summer job on the famous Sunset Strip in Hollywood. There was a cool clothing store adjacent to some of the rock clubs that catered to a music-biz clientele, and it looked like a neat place to work.

I walked in and spoke to one of the partners, but he said his associate made all of the hiring decisions, so I waited for him to show up. After a half-hour he ambled in looking unusually frisky for that time of day. He had a big grin on his face, which signaled that he had just gotten away with something.

I looked at him and he immediately laughed, "You're the boss?" I asked incredulously. He looked at his partner, wondering who I was, and the partner said, "He wants a job."

The boss said, "You want a job? You're HIRED!" And he walked away.

It turned out to be a fun position because I was left by myself to run the place. How did I know to dispense with formality when selling myself into the job? I took the measure of the place, the inventory, and the boss, and I realized that this was the least formal place on earth.

Had I tried to be a stiff applicant, the head honcho would have said to get rid of this creep! He was grinning, so I started laughing. Immediately, I picked up on the emotion in the situation, and I simply mirrored it back to the buyer.

Naturals appreciate that buyers need to be placed into a spending or an investing mood.

The retailer who hired me was already in a carefree mood. I recognized and went with it instead of snapping him out of it. A hundred people could have asked him for a job during that week, but only one got it: Me!

Case in Point: Meet My Stockbroker

Why do I keep a some of my investments with my broker at a full commission brokerage? Given that firm's high fees for purchasing securities, aren't I better off moving my assets to a discounter? Wouldn't that be the rational thing to do?

I know it is, but I LIKE MY BROKER. I'm paying a premium because I'm investing in our relationship. He makes me WANT to buy from him, and I'm sure most of his clients feel the same way I do.

But he also uses emotions in selling, and I just can't get an emotional or human payoff from my online trading activity. For example, he lights up whenever I bring my daughter in for a visit. (She's also one of his clients, and she's the best kind: Very patient!)

His excitement when he sees her could come from several emotions. He may feel GENUINE AFFECTION for her, or he could love kids and simply ENJOY them whenever he's in their presence. I know I get a big charge out of children, especially when I unexpectedly see them in a business situation.

He also uses ENTHUSIASM. For example, he is very positive about buying shares in the Walt Disney Company, and his desk is adorned with dozens of their toys. (Yes, he is a grown-up!) Ask him about Disney, and he brightens immediately.

By showing emotions so visibly, he sends a message that he can be trusted. He's not concealing anything from me, and our interests are aligned. If I buy Disney stock he'll be rooting for it and not simply calculating his commissions whether I win or lose.

Negative Emotions Can Sell

Naturals use the entire spectrum of emotions when they sell. This means they don't limit themselves to upbeat, positive themes.

If they feel they need to make a point or cut through a buyer's rationalizations, they'll use negative emotions such as FEAR. A periodontist I visited did this with me a number of months ago with tremendous effect.

By way of background, let me say I have been an ardent non-flosser. I've always felt that brushing regularly and frequent professional cleanings should be enough to keep my teeth and gums in good repair. But after an exam, the dental specialist asked me about my nonflossing philosophy.

I said:

"That's why I come in for cleanings every three months, Doc. I've delegated the plaque removal to you!"

He slowly turned to me, and then in a hushed voice, like Clint Eastwood, he asked:

"Well, how long would you like to keep your teeth?"

At first, I was stunned and just a little offended by his absurd question. I thought, "I want to keep them for as long as I live, you dummy!"

But he was dumb like a fox. In a simple question, he linked my nonflossing habit to premature tooth loss. Frankly, I didn't think the two were connected, but his inquiry said in effect:

If you don't start flossing, you will start losing your teeth!

I started flossing the next day, and I've been doing it almost without fail each and every day since. And it has made a remarkable difference in my dental health, so I'm happy about it.

Fear Appeals Can Be Very Persuasive

The message the dentist used contains a high fear appeal. Effectively, it says that if you don't do what I say, you'll end up in big trouble. In sales, it would involve a salesperson saying, "If you don't buy from me, you'll probably lose a lot of money."

Most non-natural sellers are afraid of using fear in their presentations. They're concerned that they'll seem too strident and too manipulative. They believe it is more pleasant and upbeat to stay positive, with the reasons they supply to customers for buying.

They're certainly right, in a sense, that's it's more fun to simply supply pleasant reasons for moving forward. After all, negatives can seem depressing, right?

But what non-naturals don't get is the fact that a substantial number of prospects need to be pried out of complacency, and fear can be a powerful tool for nudging them in your direction.

Non-naturals may be right about one thing, and that is the fact that some prospects RESENT the use of high fear messages. They would prefer hearing the dentist ask, "How long would you like to keep that lovely smile of yours?" which is a moderate fear appeal.

It says the same thing my dentist said but with less negativity. It can be equally effective in producing attitudinal and behavioral changes in people. The *magnitude of fear* you use is your choice.

The bottom line is that if you want to be as effective as natural born salespeople you'll need to use the full gamut of emotions in your selling. Inevitably, this will include some degree of fear.

Altruism Sells

A successful fellow who is in the multilevel marketing business came to me for some consulting help a few months ago. He has put altruism to work create a large down line of distributors who are making him wealthy.

Specifically, his group sells subscriptions to a satellite broadcasting service. One of the channels is dedicated to positive thinking programming. My client asserts that this channel is exceedingly important in helping at-risk youths see there are alternatives to drugs and self-destructive lifestyles.

Of course, he tried to recruit me into his group, and the appeal he used was a powerful one. In effect, he said:

Help me to help turn around the youth of this country!

Who could be against that idea? After all, the gun we take out of a single teenager's hand could be the one that is aimed at us or at someone we love, right? He says we can help ourselves and our nation by helping him, plus we get about 100 channels to watch for a low subscription rate!

The fellow's pitch builds upon the motivation many of us have to DO GOOD and to GIVE SOMETHING BACK TO THE COM-MUNITY. Many folks would look at what he's doing and say, "Why he has just found a novel way to sell satellite dishes!"

That's true enough, but he has accomplished something that few, if any, non-naturals could accomplish. He has intuitively found a very powerful hot button that makes normally cynical people BELIEVERS.

Naturals do this all the time, and that's why watching them work is so exciting. A great reason for buying will cascade from their lips spontaneously, and the bean counters of the sales world will be at a loss to explain how they pulled it off.

It's Like Trying to Describe a Flower with Words

I was a very new salesman at Time-Life Books when I happened upon one of these great sales breakthroughs. In the middle of describing our beautiful hard cover books to a reluctant prospect, I simply exclaimed:

"Mrs. Smith, it's like trying to describe a flower with words. These books are THAT special, so let's get you started with this series and I KNOW you'll be pleased, Okay?"

I'll never forget the moment this phrase sprouted from my mouth. My sales manager froze in his tracks as he was patrolling the phone center. I earned the sale, and he immediately boomed out:

"Did everyone hear that? 'It's like trying to describe a flower with words!' Now, THAT'S how to sell these books!"

I had simply put the emotion to work in my presentation. The result was instantaneous and magical.

Put the Power of Faith to Work

One of the best sales trainers around is Zig Ziglar. Zig started his career by selling pots and pans, and he has gone on to become a highly compensated and much admired speaker and author.

Zig is also very active in his church, and he's not timid about mentioning this fact in his books. It's no surprise that when he speaks he sounds a little like a preacher. He'll punch out the end of a line in the same way a minister will by adding something "extra-ah" so folks in the last pew can hear it.

What Zig is attuned to, as are so many natural born salespeople, is the fact that selling is sermonic. Many of the best salespeople don't deliberately emulate preachers, but they do put the power of FAITH into their presentations.

You may have heard of this phenomenon. It's sometimes referred to as BELIEVING IN YOUR PRODUCT. There's no question in my mind that this is part of the equation that naturals put to work. When I employed the phrase "like describing a flower with words," I was definitely a complete believer in the quality of the library I was selling.

But belief, alone, doesn't sell. We have to take mere belief two crucial steps farther if we want to sell like the naturals sell.

We need to transform mere belief into FAITH, and then we need to COMMUNICATE that faith to prospects.

I may be convinced that my products and services are spectacular, but unless my convictions are demonstrated before prospects, they're worthless when it comes to selling.

Naturals Project Contagious Self-Confidence

When I moved into management with Time-Life, my best rep laid down a challenge that I found irresistible.

"I can sell any book to anybody at any time!" he proclaimed.

I knew Barry very well and I suspected he could live up to his boast, but I decided to hear him out anyway.

"And to prove it," he went on, "I'll pitch a bogus library and sell it to the first prospect I speak to."

He took our very effective script for selling REAL libraries and changed some words here and there. Suddenly, he unveiled what he labeled the Industrial Library. His lead book in the series was called *Soot*.

He made the title as unattractive as possible, just to increase the challenge. I decided to let him go for it, so he quickly dialed the phone.

Within a few seconds, he was into the descriptive portion of his presentation:

"Mrs. Jones, in our lead book, Soot, *you'll see the birth of the modern machine age. You'll relive the bleak urban landscape of Dickensian England."*

It was nothing short of astonishing. Then, he effortlessly transitioned into the closing portion of the call.

"So let's get this wonderful library started for you, and I know you'll be pleased, okay?"

Mrs. Jones enthusiastically responded with her own, "Okay, Barry!"

Barry was just warming up. He quickly called another prospect. Same pitch, same result. I had to stop him because if he kept it up, we would have been on the hook to publish his new series!

What did his little demonstration prove? Yes, Barry was a creative and humorous salesman, but the single most important quality that he projected, which enabled him to sell an absurd library can be captured in one word:

Confidence

He bubbled over with this spectacular, money making quality. Confidence is one of the major strengths that all natural salespeople project. It doesn't always appear as a breast-beating, look-out-world-here-I-come sort of bravado.

When Barry wasn't tooting his own horn he could have easily been mistaken for an introverted CPA. He didn't appear flashy in any way. Yet he was a great salesperson.

What do supremely confident salespeople DO that we can emulate?

1. *They take control of the selling environment.*

For example, when I was pitching a software company on sponsoring some of my seminars, I arrived in their conference room and immediately took a seat at the head of the table.

The next thing I did was ask if I could use the white board to illustrate my points. Each of these actions sent a take charge signal that said, "I know where I'm headed and what I'm doing."

If you think these behaviors don't have an impact, consider this:

There is an acting teacher who helps executives to exude self-confidence. One of his most popular instructional units is entitled "How To Walk Into A Room."

When I questioned whether one's gait was all that important, he said:

It contributes to forming someone's first impression of us, and you know how important THAT is!

2. *Naturals seem unflappable.*

There are always things that can't be controlled during a sales presentation, but naturals don't allow these intrusions to derail them. If the phone rings in the conference room, they take it in stride and resume their talks exactly where they left off after succinctly recapping what they had said to that point.

3. *Naturals value their own time, and they show it.*

It's important for prospects to appreciate that sellers have other deals they need to attend to. Sellers make it appear that their services are in demand. They make a point of looking at their watches to send the signal that they have full agendas.

This sort of signal is a subtle warning to not waste time.

4. *They smile under pressure.*

Just like former Presidents Carter and Reagan, naturals are able to project friendliness despite the fact that they're besieged by pressures.

5. *Naturals make their fears and anxieties work for them.*

Like experienced public speakers, natural born salespeople learn to transform negative emotions into positive ones. Instead of monitoring their shortness of breath and sweaty palms as signs of debilitating fear, they perceive these as signs of excitement.

Instead of disabling themselves, they ENABLE themselves. Obstacles along the path of success are seen as stepping stones instead of stumbling blocks.

6. *They don't take delays personally.*

A prospect Jim has been working on for six months seems to be ducking his calls. When Jim finally gets him on the line, the prospect says that his firm isn't going to be able to move forward for at least three more months.

Does Jim hang up the phone and scream? Does he see the delay as a personal rebuke for his inability to close the order now?

Does he show his impatience to the buyer? No, he accepts the verdict and moves on with the cultivation and closing of other prospects. He intuitively appreciates that some deals will click right away, and others will take longer to close.

7. *They don't take no's personally.*

Three months transpire, and Joe discovers a competitor has stolen the deal from under his nose. There's no chance that his prospect will buy from him this year.

Does he feel inept, or does he lionize his competitor? No way.

He wishes his prospect well, and mentions that HE is still interested in doing business with the potential client. He cordially invites the prospect to call upon him in the future.

Not only does he not take rejections personally, but he chooses to see them as temporary.

8. *Naturals tell themselves it's a big world out there.*

No one will ever end up with 100 percent of the market in a given industry unless they have a monopoly. No salesperson can expect to win them all. In fact, in selling you only have to close a relatively small proportion of deals in order to be supremely successful.

As long as you keep pitching new prospects and your sales approach is competent, you'll emerge with your share of deals. Knowing this to your core, as naturals do, confers a sense of tranquillity and great self-confidence.

9. *Naturals stay loose.*

In a recent television commercial, actor Jack Palance touts an after-shave lotion with the question, "Isn't confidence SEXY?" That's not a careful question, is it? It's free-and-easy.

Loose, and not uptight. Watch Ken Griffey, Jr. swing at a baseball. He's a natural. His swing is fluid, and it seems like a single, effortless motion. He wouldn't hit nearly as many home runs if he tensed his muscles at the wrong times. He succeeds because he knows it doesn't really matter what pitchers throw at him.

What counts is how he chooses to respond. As long as he's loose, he's going to get a lot of big hits. Natural salespeople know this as well.

I think this is one of the reasons so many great salespeople have a sports background or are avid fans. The rhythms of victory in sports are uncannily similar to those that we find in selling.

10. *Naturals stay in the present moment.*

They don't bother with second-guessing what they just said or did, or what may have happened yesterday. Like the stock market, they realize that the world of business changes by the second, and what's happening right now means a ton more than what happened yesterday.

Their focus is placed squarely in the moment. In the NOW. Just like the counter people at Baskin Robbins ice-cream shops, they finish one customer transaction and immediately say, "Next!"

Act confidently. You'll convey your belief in what you're doing, and this will engender confidence in your prospects as well.

How Can a 98-pound Weakling Lift a 4,000-pound Car?

We've all heard stories about people who have performed extraordinary feats in urgent circumstances. Kids have been saved by frail folks who can suddenly lift cars off the ground.

How do we explain these events? We may say it's the power of adrenaline, but that's only partly true. The adrenaline was released by powerful emotions and by A PASSIONATE DESIRE to help someone in need.

Learn to turn on your passionate desire to help whenever you contact a prospect or whenever they contact you. When I was in the car leasing business, I had the great pleasure of dealing with a car dealer by the name of Allen.

I'd purchase my new cars from him, and despite the fact that he was the head honcho of his firm, he always made me want to come back because he exuded a *sincere desire to help*, as well as tons of gratitude. After quoting a price on a given vehicle, he'd end the conversation with:

"Hope I can help! Please let me know."

It always sounded to me as if he wanted to be part of the deal, no matter what. He seemed to enjoy doing business with me. Who can't like a guy like Allen while rewarding him with the lion's share of business?

Case in Point: Charles Revson

Many of the very best natural born salespeople don't concentrate upon selling products in the conventional sense of the word. At least, they don't sell the tangible components of products. Instead, they shine when they celebrate the intangible, emotional glories of their wares.

One of the most famous naturals to do this was the cosmetics giant, Charles Revson. With an uncanny sense of what his customers sincerely wanted, he didn't see himself in the business of hustling rouge, lipsticks, and facial powders.

As he so brilliantly stated, "We don't sell cosmetics. We sell hope."

This insight, and the guidance it provided, enabled Revlon to become an international powerhouse and a true industry leader. Revlon sells the hope that customers will appear more beautiful, more desirable, and that they'll consider themselves to be more worthwhile.

Revson probably appreciated that people will pay a premium for hope, but if you merely try to sell them the physical dimensions of products, you'll be doomed to charging less and less money for them.

The reason? They'll be regarded as mere commodities, like steel, aluminum, and soybeans. And the market will be won by lowest priced producer.

There is an interesting value phenomenon at work when naturals make sales.

Implicitly, naturals appreciate that people want quality, and they'll be delighted to pay a premium if they're confident they're buying the best item in its class. Some people chase the lowest prices, but if they can be convinced that they're buying junk, even they'll consider treating themselves to a better class of goods and services.

Naturals Elevate Customer Aspirations

In a sense, naturals ratchet up the aspirations of buyers in much the same way that a gifted teacher encourages his or her students to want to achieve better grades. Quality percolates up and out of great salespeople.

Through their verbal, nonverbal, and symbol manipulating behavior, the wizards of selling make people want the best, and more important, they make customers feel good about paying for the best.

Case in Point: Ralph Lauren

Naturals are quite gifted at selling what I would call the Good Life. They know that you just can't go wrong selling the American Dream in all of its manifestations.

A modern natural who does this and thrives in the rag trade, is none other than Ralph Lauren.

Walk into one of his boutiques and you'll be treated to a primer on how to sell the Good Life. You'll probably be delighted by his displays of natural products. His floors are apt to be polished woods, and his stores will usually contain furniture from the period 1920-1938.

His clothes are mostly expensive wools, cashmeres, silks, and fine Egyptian cottons. And the image he's beaming forth is one of unhurried enjoyment, studied leisure, and easy affluence.

I'm sure that when people plunk down two hundred dollars for a Polo sweatshirt they aren't buying an item that they really intend to sweat in. They buy it for the label and the image of upscale sports that Lauren purveys.

It's as if Lauren is saying, "You can look sporty, dress casually, and feel athletic without breaking a sweat or looking like a bum!"

Lauren is selling more than clothes. Once he puts his highly valued Polo pony logo on your shirt or sweater, you can walk into a fine restaurant, be treated with respect, and feel that you're going to fit in.

Ralph Lauren is really selling PERMISSION to dress casually.

As long as people know that your Polo sweater cost as much as a blazer, you can wear it nearly anywhere you may have felt obliged to wear a blazer!

Recently, Ralph Lauren went public, and his stock has been doing well. Obviously, his image of easy success and "old money" is nearly universally appealing. By inventing the Ralph Lauren Polo Club logo and product line, he has enabled anyone with a few bucks to feel he can belong to a tony club without the hassles.

Lauren is one natural who is selling luxury and exclusivity non-exclusively. It's a brilliant strategy!

Do You Sincerely Want to Be Rich?

Bernard Cornfield was a colorful natural who is credited with having popularized the mutual fund concept among individual investors. Before old Bernie happened along, folks used to pick stocks one at a time while paying high commissions for their transactions. Bernie convinced them to entrust their funds to professional money managers, and his famous sales question was:

"Do you sincerely want to be rich?"

Note that he didn't ask investors if they wanted an above-average return on their money. He didn't ask if they wanted to beat the Dow Jones Industrial Average.

He asked them for a PASSIONATE response. Not just a reaction that says, "Sure I'd like to be rich." Cornfield demanded that clients respond that they had a SINCERE desire for treasure.

That is a natural born salesperson at work. He'll inject powerful emotions into selling because he appreciates that people need to have strong desires unleashed in order to be motivated to take action immediately.

Do Naturals Really Care about What They're Doing?

So far in this chapter I've been painting a picture of naturals as individuals who can be rather intense emotionally. If you have the image of two football teammates butting helmets before taking the field, that's typically what we associate with getting psyched up for competition.

But some naturals don't wear their emotions on their sleeves. In fact, they can, at times, seem very detached from what they're doing.

Take Rick as an example. He was fortunate enough to go to work for a major high tech firm right out of his M.B.A. program. He's a smart guy but his greatest strength isn't in his intellect. He's a strong salesman because he "doesn't sweat the little stuff," as he puts it.

I've watched him over the years as he has raised capital for one losing business proposition after another. What I've marveled at is his ability to walk away unscathed from the firms that have crashed and burned while he was in the pilot's seat.

He just doesn't allow himself to become stigmatized by failure. At first I thought he might have been acting too callously about the misfortunes of his investors, of whom, I was gratefully not one.

But then I reassessed what he was doing emotionally. He wasn't acting in a CARELESS or negligent way. He was intentionally living his life, and taking his career lumps in a CAREFREE way. And, as you can imagine, there is a huge difference between these emotions.

If we are too careless, prospects will pick up on our detachment and they'll mirror it right back to us. In Southern California, I see people who come across this way all the time.

Many of them are aspiring actors who forget to get into their current roles as they wait tables in restaurants or work behind the counter at Sears. They purposely seem to be sending signals that say, "I'm not really a waiter or a clerk. I'm a future Academy Award winner!"

People who come across as being carefree actually encourage customers to relax and get into a buying mood. If a salesperson seems like he's enjoying his role and his life, there must be something right about his product. This is the inference most prospects will make.

Naturals Avoid Being Uptight

I think it will be easier to appreciate a carefree manner if we contrast it with its opposite: being uptight. Uptight salespeople can literally care too much about whether customers are going to buy. Consequently, they come across as needy and out for themselves.

You know the feeling. You walk into shop just to check out the current selection of wares and the salesperson looks at you with a wolf's stare. It's as if YOU are his next meal!

An overly serious salesperson can literally scare away business if he acts this way. Moreover, by seeming self-absorbed and out for himself, he induces customers to mirror these miserly traits right back to him.

In other words, when someone seems to be reaching for our wallets, our hand reflexively tries to stymie his attempt. It's a simple, animalistic mode of self-protection.

On the other hand, when a salesperson seems carefree, she'll often invest time with us and project a sense of *abundance*. When we feel there's more than enough for everyone, we're in the right mood to buy.

T.S. Eliot, the great poet, summed up the right emotional stance to adopt when he said:

"Teach us to care, and teach us not to care."

Try to Play Loose

We should be interested in sales outcomes, but we can't allow ourselves to grow uptight about them. Maintaining the right amount of emotional detachment is something that naturals are masterful at doing, and we'd be wise to imitate this strength.

When I was watching the recent baseball pennant race, announcer Vin Scully of the Dodgers, made an interesting observation. He said that teams that were no longer competing for the postseason playoffs were the "most dangerous opponents" for contenders to face.

How come? Vinny said, "They have nothing to lose, and they're really playing loose. They're just playing for fun."

I think this describes the attitudes of naturals. They feel loose almost all the time. They don't choke under pressure as so many athletes and teams do in their attempts to win championships.

This translates into some interesting comments that naturals make about their careers. Bob, a software salesman, said to me, "You know, if they fired me tomorrow, I'd probably still come in every day just to watch the action. In fact, I might even PAY THEM for the privilege to watch!"

Enter the Winner's Zone

Speaking of athletes and competition, I'd be less than thorough if I didn't explore, however briefly, the concept of the zone.

The zone is a psychological state that athletes, salespeople, and others enter when they are performing especially well. It is like a state of grace that descends upon you, and when you're in it, you feel you can do no wrong.

We've all enjoyed in-zone experiences. Mine date back to my Little League days. When I was ten, I had a tremendous tryout day. I just knew, deep down in my bones that I was going to do something exceptional.

When I was asked to show my stuff in the field, I was asked to chase a fly ball. The coach who hit mine hit it so hard that he thought it was impossible to catch. Immediately after the bat struck the ball he cried out, "Forget it!"

But I was already turned around and running full speed after it. I prayed to have a great tryout and to stun the crowd, and here was my chance to do it.

I kept running, extended my body, and shot out my arm like a harpoon. Miraculously, I reeled in the ball. A huge "WOW!" burst from my peers stationed on the sidelines, and then applause.

That day my best friend, Bobby, made the Cardinals, and I was assigned to the Dodgers. He was a pitcher, and I was a catcher. I boasted to him, "The first time I face you, I'm going to hit a home run over the center field fence, just like Babe Ruth!"

"Sure, Goodman, sure."

A year later, as a tight game was about to draw to a close, Bobby was brought in as a relief pitcher to face me. I smiled broadly while pointing to center field. He suppressed a grin.

On a two-and-one count, I reached for an outside pitch and launched a rocket into dead center field. It hung in the air, seemingly forever, and then it dropped outside the fence for a home run.

Bobby couldn't believe it.

I knew it would happen. I had rehearsed it a hundred times in my imagination.

Natural born salespeople embody the same feeling of certainty about their efforts. But more important than simply finding themselves in the zone, they're capable of putting themselves into the zone when they need to go there.

There's a time when it pays off very handsomely to enter this special psychological and emotional arena: when you're discussing prices with customers.

When I first became a consultant, I had no idea as to what my on-site training fees should be. People attended my college-sponsored seminars and very frequently they'd stay after to inquire about my doing a speech or a seminar for their companies.

At first, I was a little unsure of what the market would bear. But after a while, I transformed negotiating into a fun game. I set my fees, and I purposely tried to make them sound exceedingly reasonable when quoting them.

If prospects questioned how I arrived at my figures, I'd smile and calmly explain how middle-of-the-road they really were. By projecting utter tranquillity about money matters I was able to get my prospects to relax and see the reasonableness of my charges.

Once they saw that I was "okay" with my fees, they became okay with them as well. Naturals can get away with charging premium prices and fees and maintaining healthy profit margins because they come across naturally when justifying them.

David Will Almost Always Beat Goliath

The leasing company I worked for decided to grow its customer base through acquisitions. It seemed like a sound strategy. Take over a firm, inherit existing leases, and then resign customers by offering to pull clients out of their older cars early before their original leases terminated.

We said, "I can put you into a new car at no extra cost to you if you act NOW!" Not a bad appeal, especially to people who live in their cars like many lessees.

But there was something that put a crimp into this well considered plan. Customers of the acquired firms were unusually loyal to their former salespeople who were let go when the big company swallowed up their employers.

My task was to get the old customers to renew their leases or to sign new ones with the new firm. What I didn't anticipate was the inoculation that the old salespeople gave to their clients.

I discovered that they used a very powerful emotional appeal to keep their customers on their side as they landed at new leasing companies. They characterized my firm as being big, callous, and uncaring. They said we were much too institutional to deliver the personal treatment that clients had enjoyed with the smaller firm.

And, sooner or later, we were going to pass along the costs of acquiring the little firm to the customers in the form of higher lease rates and numerous hidden costs.

This was nothing less than a brilliant sales strategy that the naturals at the smaller company hatched. It was a modern equivalent of David versus Goliath, and most goodhearted customers unconsciously root for the underdog in such lopsided contests.

The more I tried to fight back against the accusations of the displaced salespeople, the more sympathetic they seemed to be to their steady customers. The reason? It seemed like I was kicking poor David when he was down on his knees.

Use Emotional Archetypes

I offer this example to demonstrate that naturals use emotional archetypes, or well known images, when they sell. They may not consciously label their efforts "The David versus Goliath Routine," but they unconsciously know what they're doing.

They're appealing directly to the sympathies and the emotions of their buyers. An archetype is a persuasive formula that owes its power to the fact that most of us know certain stories that have been passed down through the millennia.

To be persuaded by these legends and references, all we have to do is be exposed to a part of them by a seller. Then, we'll supply the missing context that contains the moral to the story.

David and Goliath is a dynamic and vivid Biblical story. There are many, many others. If I wanted to counter the leasing salespersons' myth, I might say to my clients:

"I'm sure you'll find that this is a change for the better, and we'll offer you benefits they simply can't offer. So, why look backward when we can look forward to better things?"

What Biblical person looked back and paid a huge price for doing so? If you said Lot's wife, you're right! She turned to a pillar of salt for looking back.

Satchel Paige, the wonderful pitcher, once echoed this Biblical reference when he said, "Don't look back, something might be gaining on you!"

The person who loses by focusing upon the past instead of the present and future is an archetype of foolishness and failure. It is a person who doubts instead of one who believes.

Naturals use this story and other archetypes as a sort of emotional shorthand to get prospects to buy.

There are many brief sayings that accomplish the same outcome. Here are a few common ones:

Pennywise and pound foolish
Better safe, than sorry
You get what you pay for
Nobody ever got fired for buying I.B.M.
A guarantee is only as strong as the company that's behind it
Watch the pennies, and the dollars will take care of themselves
A little bit of knowledge is a dangerous thing

What If He's Hit By a Bus?

Naturals don't rely only upon folklore and accepted aphorisms to do their persuading. They also draw from their own rich experiences to formulate their own archetypes. Once, I did this after missing out on a big deal.

I pitched Flying Tigers, the air freight company, on doing a nationwide customer service training program. I intended to personally conduct the training at their many airport locations.

I was selling to a manager who was also considering other vendors, including Xerox Learning Systems. At that time, XLS, as it was known, had a sparkling corporate image, and large companies often like to do business with other biggies.

XLS learned that I was trying to get the contract, so according to my Tigers contact, they used an emotional appeal to knock me out of contention. They said, "He has a good reputation, but he's only one guy, right? What if he's half way through the program and he's hit by a bus?"

Interesting fear message, right? Well, my contact at Tigers passed on these words to me, and what could I say in response? That I cross streets very carefully?

I had no suitable answer, but I developed one a few years later. As it turned out, Xerox Learning Systems, as well as Flying Tigers, both DIED in a corporate sense before me! XLS was sold to another corporation, and Tigers was gobbled up by Federal Express.

Guess what? Whenever I am confronted by a similar competitive situation where my adversaries are characterizing me as a one man band while painting pictures of my imminent demise, I tell prospects the Tigers/Xerox story.

Additionally, I throw in for good measure the fact that shortly after the Tigers competition, Xerox actually hired me to train its own sales and service personnel!

One more thing: I learned that an executive's life can be insured. In other words, if a client wants to hire me to do a huge contract, I can eliminate its risk by insuring my life while making the firm a beneficiary of the policy.

So, when a prospect challenges, "What if you die?", I counter with, "My competitors will probably predecease ME, just like XLS and Flying Tigers."

And, of course I'm appealing to another Biblical image when I'm saying this, "The meek shall inherit the earth."

(And if not the earth, we might eke out enough contracts to fight the next battle.)

Enthusiasm Is the Highest Paid Emotion in the World

Recently, I spoke to a reader of one of my bestsellers, *You Can Sell Anything By Telephone!* He wanted to buy another one of my books so I handled the transaction.

Before he left the line, he mentioned that he was starting a new telemarketing department, and then he paused. Into that gap I inserted the word, "Great!"

My voice peaked, which sent a signal that I thought starting a new department was a fine idea. I transmitted a signal that told him that he'd probably be successful with this undertaking.

Just then, he replied:

"Would you enclose some information about your consulting? I'd like to use your services to help me to get going."

"Be glad to," I said. I also pointed out how he'd benefit from purchasing my audio seminar called "The New Telemarketing™." There's no question in my mind that he'll examine my brochure and invest in the tapes for his next purchase.

What caused his rapid acceleration of interest in my goods and services? Yes, he liked my *You Can Sell...* book, and the value he received from it provided a justification for his inquiry about other books.

But what really hooked him was the simple fact that I reacted enthusiastically to his plans.

If my tone of voice had merely come across as flat, or if I said, "That's nice," or merely "Okay," when he said he was starting a telemarketing unit, I doubt very much if he would have expressed such interest in my other wares.

Let me say this another way:

My enthusiasm FOR HIM made him enthusiastic ABOUT ME!

You know from your own personal life that enthusiasm is contagious. Just watch man's best friend, the mutt, at work.

Dogs wholeheartedly wag their tales, and some claim they even grin when their human companions enter their company. Canines brighten markedly when we enter a room. Seeing them have this overwhelming, "I like you" reaction, we beam it right back to them.

You would think that we humans would take a lesson from dogs, who have to be the biggest success story among non-human species. Their only product is enthusiasm, along with a slurpy kiss every now and then.

Yet millions and millions of us wouldn't consider spending the rest of our lives without these wonderful buddies.

I suspect that salespeople who do try to project enthusiasm miss the mark, though they have no idea how they're erring. They mistakenly express enthusiasm toward the features of their products instead of toward their customers as human beings.

Naturals sell prospects on the value of the prospects: themselves. This makes a huge impact upon one's effectiveness. There are several consulting contracts I have been awarded because I expressed genuine appreciation for the quality of the firm that my prospects were working for.

One company, a unit of American Express, was easy to admire. It treated its employees very generously, and when I persuaded my contacts to discuss how enamored they were with their own employer, I resold them on their wisdom in selecting such a fine entity with which to become professionally associated.

Implicitly, I was saying I would be proud to have American Express as a client. And my buoyed up prospects gladly helped to make that come true.

Ten Steps for Becoming Perennially Enthusiastic

Enthusiasm is one our most precious emotions. Nearly anything great can be accomplished with enthusiasm. And little of any consequence is created without it.

Having said that, how can we become enthusiastic, and more important, how can we stay that way? Here are my ten tips for staying upbeat, positive, and in the winner's circle.

1. *Remember where you came from.* When I was growing up, I couldn't wait to get into the business world. To me, being on my own earning a paycheck was the greatest thing that could happen to anyone.

What kid doesn't want a feeling of self-control and an unlimited cash flow? Well, I wanted it all, and when I started out I was literally, penniless.

I worked as a busboy, a box boy, sold newspapers on corners, and my very first job out of high school was delivering FISH in a sweltering truck. Nonetheless, this enabled me to rent a one room apartment and start working my way through college.

A pound of ground beef, which I'd cook to perfection on my hot plate, was the picture of luxury and heaven to a still growing eighteen year old. This is where I come from.

And when I start to get down, I remember that kid and smile and think that if this is how far I've come already, imagine where I can go!

2. *Remember friends who didn't make it.* One of my best friends from grade school made a few wrong turns with his life and ended up gunned down by gangsters when he was just eighteen. At high school reunions, we all still reminisce about Doug and how wasted his life was.

You never know when your time is up, even if you're saint, so make years of enjoyment out of your days.

3. *No matter how low you get, remember that others have been lower still and climbed out of their ruts.* Never give up on yourself or your potential. Keep telling yourself good things about you and all you've done to make the world better.

4. *You might be missing a small success ingredient, and if you keep plodding along you'll find it.* I can't tell you how many times things have looked bleak for my business, only to find that when things were darkest, a new beginning was waiting just around the corner.

5. *Make sure to make a profit from your loss.* Every setback contains valuable lessons. If you look at the lives of great achievers, you'll see a pattern of failure that precedes their successes. Some very rich people have gone broke several times before reaching a durable level of financial success.

6. *Take noble risks.* Try new strategies for solving old problems. Don't let yourself get complacent by trying not to lose. It's impossible to avoid all risks, because life itself involves ceaseless risks, many of which we're not consciously aware of.

7. *Count your blessings.* We're so lucky to have bodies with parts that are in good working condition. Lots of people aren't as lucky as we are. Even temporary maladies can teach us lessons. When I was on the stump doing countless seminars, I'd often get laryngitis, which would force me to speak less. Sometimes, I'd be lecturing with only a whisper and hand gestures. Each time this has happened I've recovered with a sense of elation about my ability to communicate through the voice.

How precious a gift this is! How often we waste words with petty comments or garbage thoughts. If we had a meter that restricted our daily allowance of words, we'd be a lot wiser in how we chose to use them, and we'd be much more grateful that this is one of many gifts we enjoy.

8. *Do, right now, exactly what you fear.* Fear is like a bad partner in business who is constantly wearing you down and wasting your emotional and financial assets. Fear keeps most of us from enjoying life and our jobs to the fullest.

Are you afraid of public speaking? You know the antidote for that, don't you? Force yourself to speak to groups as often as you can. Through systematic desensitization, you can condition yourself right out of your fears.

And once you have witnessed yourself conquering a given phobia, your confidence will soar and you'll want to overcome others. Who knows, you just might become a daredevil!

9. *Innovate.* Do things differently. I'll take this suggestion to extreme limits. For instance, when I'm in strange territory such as a new town and I've rented a car, I don't mind getting a little lost. What do I mean by a little?

Well, if I'm in the right zip code, I think meandering around is a good idea. I get to see new things and I get new ideas.

Or, I'll take a bus to get to a seminar site instead of taking a taxi or private car. Just the fact that I've shaken myself out of ordinary patterns helps me to see new things, and to see old things in new ways. That's what innovating is all about.

10. *Don't worry about feeling low or getting periodically negative.* You could be priming yourself for some radical change of the good kind. Often, that sinking feeling, or anger, or disgust with one's present circumstances will be just the incentive you need to get off the dime and change for the better.

Welcome the downs so you can revel in the inevitable ups.

One of my all-time favorite movies is the classic, It's a Wonderful Life, starring Jimmy Stewart. He plays a fellow who got down on himself so much that he was about to end it all. An angel rescued him by showing him what the world would have been like if he had never existed, and a sorry place it was. Stewart's character rebounded from gloom and celebrated his life, problems and all.

While there are many lessons in the movie, I think one stands out above all. No matter how gloomy things might seem, there is light breaking on the horizon. Hang in there long enough and you'll be warmed by its glow.

While many salespeople are afraid of using emotions in their presentations, natural born salespeople seek new ways to put the passions to work as you've seen in this chapter.

In the chapter that follows, I'll show you how the best of the best use another secret weapon in their sales battles. You'll learn how to make your body language an impressive ally and silent salesperson.

CHAPTER 5

MAKE
YOUR BODY
DO YOUR
SELLING

Natural born salespeople don't communicate with words alone. *You need to learn how to use vocal tones, facial expressions, and the selling environment to cut through resistance and win sales.*

Naturally talented salespeople use a number of nonlinguistic messages that are generally referred to as body language. These include:

- hand gestures
- posture
- interpersonal distance (body bubbles)
- facial expressions
- eye contact
- vocal tones
- silence
- status symbols (object language)
- fragrances (perfumes)

In this chapter, we'll examine what naturals do, often unconsciously, which gives them the winning edge. You'll learn how to communicate through many channels and to multiply your persuasiveness.

Before we begin, I should mention that nonverbal communication has grown into a respected and very interesting field of study. Numerous people in universities perform nonverbal communication research.

In fact, a while back I taught a semester-length, credit-bearing class in this area at California State University, Northridge. So if you wish to pursue more information in this area, I think you'll be able to uncover quite a lot.

Look at How Real Sellers and Real Buyers Behave

I became interested in unraveling the secrets of using nonverbal communication when I was in the car leasing business. As an account executive, I had to participate in a ceremony that nearly always resulted in major blowouts with customers.

It occurred when a car was coming off of lease and my company needed to perform an official appraisal of body damage. After having been driven for 24, 36, or even 48 months, most vehicles were by that time very used. They bore the typical scars of road life: bald tires, body dents, and door dings from being sardined between other cars in parking lots. To their drivers, these autos were in still in mint condition. That's where our interpersonal problems with clients arose.

Lessees were usually jubilant when their leases began because they were provided with shiny new coaches that just begged to be driven. But the same leases that enabled folks to drive off the lot for only the first month's rental payment and a security deposit also required customers to bring cars back in excellent condition. Cars had to be returned with at least 50 percent tread wear remaining on the tires, without dings or major scratches, and under the prespecified mileage allowances.

For drivers who failed to meet these end of the lease standards, the penalties could easily extend into the thousands of dollars. This seemed unfair because most drivers assumed door dings and torn upholstery constituted normal wear and tear and were allowable.

What the drivers didn't appreciate was the fact that the leasing company would need to sell their car, and if it was in shoddy condition, it wouldn't bring the anticipated amount.

So appraisals would be performed, and my duty was to break the bad news to clients that they needed to write big fat checks before they could lease another car or keep a clean credit record.

It wasn't a happy circumstance, and it didn't put my customers into a devil-may-care, Oh, gosh—let's lease another car! mood. Quite the opposite; they were royally pissed off. Finally, I grew tired of these sour encounters and resolved to do something to reduce the conflict.

Furniture Arrangements and Sales Outcomes

Like most salespeople, I worked in a cubicle furnished with a desk and three chairs. One chair was located behind the desk, and two guest chairs faced the desk. It wasn't fancy.

At appraisal time, I sensed that my furniture set up was really like a barricade with rebellious customers on one side, and the establishment's force—little, old me—on the other side.

When we disagreed about appraisals, customers would lean back and create even more distance between us. Nonverbally, they were making me a stranger, an enemy, and it was next to impossible to collect the moneys that were due and retain good will in that atmosphere.

One day, it hit me that the uncomfortable scenes that we were playing didn't have to be staged the traditional way. I could do something with body language that would prevent ill will and make me seem more sympathetic.

My adjustment was so simple that now, in retrospect, I wonder why other salespeople hadn't thought of it. The next time an appraisal was handed to me I got up from behind my desk and took a chair next to my customer.

That's it!

And can you guess what happened next? Our voices took on a softer quality because we were stationed right next to each other and it wouldn't have been appropriate to have raised our voices.

So the hostility was reduced from a reduction in our vocal volume. It was as if we were discovering the contents of the appraisal at the same time. We were on a level playing field and could walk through the damage together.

I'll never forget what one customer said to me, after we handled the appraisal this way:

"Well, Gary, I'm not happy having to pay so much money, but at least I know YOU'RE ON MY SIDE!"

He was absolutely right. I was physically on his side, and this gave rise to the perception that I was attitudinally on his side as well. It was a huge confirmation for me that I had devised a nonverbal technique for persuasion that was amazingly powerful.

With this simple gesture I collected more money with fewer arguments and retained more customers than ever before.

And this is what naturals do all the time. They use their environments, their body bubbles, voices, gestures, and facial expressions in productive ways to send persuasive messages to prospects and to clients.

May I Have a Glass of Water, Please?

When Jim was only a teenager, he lost his father. So he became the man of the house when he was still in high school. He had to support his mother and clothe and feed himself, and the only way he could do it was by entering the field of sales. But he had what seemed like an overwhelming handicap: He was afflicted with a terrible stutter.

How could he sell encyclopedias door-to-door when it might take him several seconds just to say hello? Would the people he called on in his working-class neighborhood have any patience with a mere kid who had difficulty communicating?

He intuitively recognized that he had to MAKE THEM LISTEN!

But how could he, when the typical tendency for nonstutterers was to rush people like Jim by trying to finish their sentences? How could Jim transform his weakness into a strength?

He thought through his problem and resolved to control the pacing of his sales presentations. So after introducing himself and giving a brief overview of his product, he asked the head of the household:

May I have a glass of water, please?

What Jim found was that his modest request was always granted and that prospects became friendlier and more patient with him. By extending a small gesture of hospitality, buyers suddenly felt a connection to the young salesperson, and they then felt committed to being patient so he could complete his presentation.

Jim found by reaching for the water at various intervals he could control the pacing of the discussion and calm himself down, especially before answering objections.

To the surprise of nearly everyone, he became a sales leader. And by making himself sell, he actually developed the capability to control his stuttering.

Naturals frequently induce prospects to become sales assistants. Whether they ask for water, a pen, or ask customers to hold a piece of paper or a brochure, they are deputizing their prospects so that potential buyers become involved in helping the seller to succeed.

This is also a form of nonverbal communication known as object language. By using various props and physical tools, naturals take control of selling environments.

The request for a glass of water is a very clever device. Wouldn't it be psychologically inconsistent for prospects to help someone and then argue with them or give them a rough time? Also, by drinking their water, Jim was doing the symbolic equivalent of breaking bread with his prospects, and this nonverbal activity put them on common ground.

It reduced resistance while paving the way to more sales

Decorations Are Selling Props

When walking into someone's office, what are the first things you see after the desk and possibly various tools like phones, fax machines, and computers? What's hanging on the walls and squirreled into bookshelves?

You'll see memorabilia, family photographs, and other furnishings that reflect the personal life of the person. Salespeople take care to place objects around that tell guests that they're winners.

What will you see in the office of the best sellers? There will be plaques, blue ribbons, and trophies attesting to the individuals' selling prowess. Naturals will also put other items on the walls that say you're smart to be buying from me!

What could these be? Testimonials, not only from internal sources such as the president and head honchos of their firms, but also display framed pats on the back from thrilled customers.

Before greeting their prospects, naturals will often do a little staging with the help of their associates. Prospects will be led into the natural's office and left to themselves for a few minutes for the precise reason that this will provide them with the opportunity and motivation to gaze around at all of the success symbols that are present.

The concept is simple: Your selling environment should position you as a great person with whom to do business. If you can get a hold of a framed document that certifies you as a member of the HUNDRED MILLION DOLLAR CLUB or a similar distinction, then play it up!

The beauty of object language is the fact that you don't have to VOCALLY say anything. Your silent salespeople will be doing that for you. They'll make or reinforce the right impressions.

Case in Point: Impressing Potential Customers

How far should you go in designing your office so it will impress prospects? There are several show business law firms that recruit associates and provide them with a decorating allowance that can reach $75,000 depending upon their experience and their salaries.

What do they do with all of this dough? They use an interior decorator who specializes in making offices ooze with prestige. Does it pay off for the firm?

You bet. A client is much less likely to question a statement with $400 per hour billing rates if they can actually SEE where the money is going. By investing in atmospherics that might be labeled business opulent, the partners give the impression that they're worth every penny.

At the same time, when occupants look around at their environment, they're reminding themselves that they're top notch professionals.

Sometimes Downplaying Wealth Is Better

Of course, if you bandy about too many success symbols, you could turn off certain buyers. You really need to know your customers very well to determine which objects to use and which ones you should save for your personal enjoyment after hours.

Case in Point: The Beige Station Wagon

One of my leasing customers was adamant about having me obtain a white Chevy wagon for him. I searched the entire city, and the only one I could find was one in beige.

I apologized and said, "Beige is close to white, so what's the difference?" He hesitated a long time, and then he relented.

"Okay, get me the beige one."

And that's just what I did. I phoned the Chevrolet dealer, issued a purchase order, and told them to deliver it to my office where I would then complete the paperwork and help my happy client drive it away.

As you can guess, it didn't work out that smoothly. Instead, I found myself trying to calm down a super-angry lessee who gave me an impressive tutorial about how his customers think.

First of all, upon seeing the wagon he hated it. "You said it was beige!" he shouted. "It is beige," I responded, surprised and flustered.

"That's not beige. It's PISS YELLOW!" he countered.

I have to admit the car did have a yellow cast to it, but Chevy still referred to it as beige, and I showed him the official color chip to prove it.

Catching my breath, I wanted to find out why the color was so critical. After all, this was going to be used for business and not for pleasure.

Here's what he told me:

"Gary, this car looks too rich. I sell sprinkler systems to FARMERS, and they're bedrock conservative. If I drive up in a simple white wagon, they'll think nothing of it. Hell, they won't even know whether it's new or old. But If I show them anything too flashy, they'll think my prices are too high and that I'm making too much on them."

He tried to get me to send it back to the dealer, but I told him it was too late. I had already bought it. So we both looked down for several minutes, and I used another nonverbal technique that helped me get out of the jam.

I Simply Kept My Big Mouth Shut!

There's an old expression in selling that points to the power of certain nonverbal manipulations. With my leasing client, this one popped into my mind at the crucial time:

When there's a long silence between a seller and buyer, he who speaks first LOSES!

Remember where we were in this process. The buyer said, "Send it back!" and I said, "I can't. It's yours. I already bought it and paid for it."

Then, he looked down, and I decided to look down as well. It was like we were counting ants or something! I wanted to speak, to say anything, to end this loud silence between us. But I remembered my training:

If you're tempted to speak first, bite your lip until it bleeds! DON'T DO IT!

I stayed mum, and he broke the silence. "Okay, I'll take it. But I still think it's PISS YELLOW!"

Why Did I Cast My Gaze Downward?

One of the sayings you'll encounter when you study body language is: "You cannot, NOT communicate." In other words, every gesture and every facial expression communicates something despite the fact that you may not want it to.

In poker, some players try to avoid telegraphing when they have a good or bad hand. By maintaining a stone-like appearance, they intentionally try to withhold information about the quality of their cards.

Some are better at this than others. Bad players are like dogs, if they're happy with a hand, they'll wag their tails. These nonverbal giveaways are known as tells.

When excited, some players will scratch their noses or tap the table with their fingers. Others may actually arch their eyebrows and start humming in a carefree manner.

What I did with my leasing customer was intentional. He looked down, and I decided to mirror him to create rapport. But by casting my eyes downward I was also intentionally trying to communicate several things to him:

1. *I'm as disappointed as you are that beige turned out to be more yellow than white.*

2. *I'm not challenging you to a stare down, because I don't want to create a macho problem by seeming too aggressive or too tough.*

3. *I'm giving you the power to be magnanimous and to help both of us save face. Only you can get us out of this impasse.*

It worked, but he did get in that last dig about being right in labeling it an unpleasant shade of yellow. Given the alternatives, the situation could have become much worse.

Making Eye Contact with Customers

We just covered an exception to the general rule about making or sustaining eye contact. Generally, you should look directly into a customer's eyes for several reasons.

First, it makes you seem sincere and genuine. How many times have you heard someone say that nobody can look me in the eye and lie at the same time?

We associate visual directness with truthfulness. Who don't we trust? People who seem shifty eyed and those who don't look us straight in the eye.

But there's another reason to use plenty of eye contact: people think we like them more when we spend more time looking into their eyes. And when they do invest this sort of attention in us, we like them more in return.

Experiments have been performed where two people are seated in front of an interviewer who spends twice as much time looking at subject A versus subject B. Invariably, A will like the interviewer better than B.

If you're not used to communicating directly through eye contact, this would be a good time to start. Before leaving this topic, there's something that I want to point out that naturals do that others don't do, which makes a huge difference in racking up sales:

Naturals SMILE through their eyes.

They seem to have a gleam in their eyes that says to prospects, "I like you and I approve of what you're saying."

If you have children, you know the look because it is similar to the expression you have when you view them. It's appreciative, gleeful, and positively expectant. This leads me to my next nonverbal subject: smiling.

When You're Smiling, the Whole World Will Buy from You!

Do you know the song, "When You're Smiling," which says that when you wear this expression life goes a lot better and the whole world smiles with you? There's truth in this.

Smiling is very, very powerful. First of all, it makes you, the wearer, feel better. When you manifest a pleasant expression you can't help but lift your spirits.

The pioneering psychologist, William James, noticed this fact, and he was one of the first people to say that if you act in a certain manner, the emotion associated with that manner will soon follow.

So act happy, and you'll become happy.

You'll spread sunshine to your prospects as well. Do you know how difficult it is not to smile when someone is smiling at you? Really, it's hard.

Just think back to when the class clown in school would start to giggle. Wasn't it contagious? And the less you wanted to smile back, the more you just had to?

We're programmed from birth to smile back at those who smile at us, whether they're parents, caregivers, or well wishers. And what happens when we smile? That's right, we feel better, and we're suddenly put into a buying mood.

Naturals smile a great deal. It gives them a tremendous non-verbal sales tool.

But what if you don't like your smile?

Fix it! I'm serious.

My daughter noticed that my coffee-bathed teeth were getting yellow, and she didn't hesitate to tell me. (Thank goodness she didn't tell me what SHADE of yellow they were getting!)

I went to a dentist who specializes in cosmetic treatments, and he prescribed a whitener, which I used over a three week period.

The results were amazing! Not only are my teeth whiter but I'm smiling a lot more, and people are smiling back. I'm suddenly aware of how I was unconsciously smiling less because I didn't like my smile.

Even if you need braces, implants, or other work, I suggest you consider investing in your smile. One psychologist says that having a better smile is the cheapest and best form of cosmetic self-improvement there is.

Should You Talk with Your Hands?

Hand gestures are also wonderful nonverbal tools if we use them well. They can emphasize what we're saying vocally. They can also regulate conversations by signaling that we have just one more thing to say.

Gestures can also demonstrate very quickly what words can only superficially communicate. If someone asks us, "How tall was he?" We can guess the height in feet and inches, or we can much more rapidly point to our chins and respond, "He came to about here."

But gestures can also be misused and constitute a distraction. If they use us, instead of our using them, it is as ungainly as a tail wagging a dog. If you notice that your clients spend too much time watching your hands instead of looking you in the eye, this is a tip off that your movements are diminishing instead of helping your effectiveness.

It could be that those folks grew up in families that admonished them to not talk with their hands. So when they see someone else using distracting gestures, they react sternly as their parents would in their place.

I think using gestures is inevitable, if only because words occasionally fail to come forth when we need them. We fill pauses with gestures to help us to reel out our reluctant sentences.

If you're not sure whether your gestures are appropriate, you can do several things. Take an interpersonal communication class at a local college where the instructor uses videotape to assist in providing feedback. If you have your own equipment, you can set it up and work without an instructor.

Should You Touch Your Prospects?

Business people seem to touch each other all the time. Sometimes it's proper, and actually expected, and other times it is uninvited and not welcomed. The topic of touching is a TOUCHY one. Sometimes it advances business relationships, and other times it sends participants into a full retreat.

The problem with touching is that it can communicate and miscommunicate many things. A handshake is almost always proper, and perceived as such, though some women still prefer not to shake hands.

You can also shake hands TOO OFTEN with a prospect, which actually has the effect of saying, that you're still at an introductory stage of your relationship.

For example, if you have been dealing with a customer for a long period of time, it may seem unusual if you said both hello and good-bye with a handshake. In other words, it could seem stiff and stilted.

What do you think about putting your hand on a customer's shoulder? Is that too intimate, and can its meaning be misconstrued?

Generally, I think so, unless you have known the person for a very long time and you're exceedingly comfortable with each other. But even then, I'm concerned that you might be seen as taking liberties with the person's private self.

In opposite-sex settings, touching can very easily be categorized as flirtation, or worse, as harassment. I have a hard time conceptualizing when this sort of conduct would appear to a bystander, colleague, or boss as innocent and appropriate, so I'd eliminate it from your body language vocabulary.

Remember: Time Talks and Space Speaks

Time and space are additional variables that send messages to customers that reflect upon you and your professionalism. What can you say, for example, about a salesperson who almost always appears to be running late?

Is this individual sending a message to his prospects? If so, what is that message saying? That he's too busy, that the prospect is unimportant, or that the seller is insensitive and uncaring?

Lateness and our general use of the clock speaks volumes about us whether we like it or not.

Case in Point: Time Talks

Marshall decided to use Acme Baskets because they had a good reputation for delivering products on time. But he found that their shipments started running late, and when he asked customer service what was wrong, they gave him vague explanations.

He found that his phone calls were returned, if at all, in the very late afternoon. By that time his blood had boiled, and he was ready to find other vendors.

Marshall interpreted Acme's slippage this way: (1) he felt his business was not important to them because his shipments seemed to go out last; and (2) he felt his requests for call backs were put on the bottom of the pile because Acme didn't really like to do business with little companies, such as Marshall's.

So he decided to shop for bids from other vendors and to jettison Acme.

Time talked to Marshall, as it talks to all of us.

None other than the great football coach, Vince Lombardi, suggested that salespeople adopt what he called Lombardi time. Lombardi time means showing up fifteen minutes EARLY for each and every sales appointment. Why do this? It shows you're a good time manager and that you're eager for your prospect's business.

Our use of space also speaks to prospects. How much distance customers maintain between themselves and us can tell us volumes about how they regard us and about the likelihood of getting or keeping their business.

If they're suddenly standoffish, and distant, there may be trouble brewing and naturals read these body signals as invitations to ask customers more about their situations to ferret out problems before it's too late.

Choose Your Selling Environment Carefully

If you ask retirees what they miss most about their former jobs, the first answer that pops out isn't the money or the status.

"It's the gossip," says management guru and octogenarian Peter Drucker. Retirees feel left out of the communication loop.

For many salespeople, work is an important social environment as well as a place to earn a paycheck. Making friends, comparing notes about life, and celebrating birthdays and employment anniversaries are rituals that give people a sense of meaning and belonging.

Naturals may be unusually gifted sellers, but they're also people who, by nature, are social creatures. You should ask yourself how much of a social component you need to have to feel fulfilled in your selling environment.

Would you prefer to do your telephone prospecting in a bullpen where you're surrounded by other salespeople, or would you prefer to be off on the sidelines sequestered into a private office? Your decision will play a major role when it comes to making or breaking your mood and your concentration.

Some sellers make better calls in a bullpen environment rather than off by themselves on the sidelines in separate offices. They sell more when they're surrounded by peers. And when they're off somewhere by themselves they feel out of touch and their productivity plummets.

Telecommuters sometimes complain of loneliness when they work from home far from the water cooler chitchat. They identify less with company goals than their on-site peers and feel more as if they work for themselves.

If you're used to being an inside salesperson and are suddenly promoted to the field, where you work out of your home, you can also experience a decline in effectiveness.

Working alone can create a feeling of anomie, or alienation. Without the formal and informal controls that come from working in the company of others, salespeople can feel unguided and out of synch. Left to create and to sustain their own work routines, they can waste time with minutia simply because they don't have peer or management pressure to perform otherwise.

Some salespeople like the camaraderie and stimulation of making calls from a bullpen. They also feel surges of competition, which propel them on to making the next call and the one after that.

And surprisingly, they frequently report feeling less self-conscious when they're pitching in a group. It feels "like a team sport," one salesperson explained to me at a seminar.

You may be different, and you may find that your calls take on a greater sense of intimacy when you're making them from behind a closed door. If you're not sure how you perform better, try both and track your results.

Compare the differences. You may be surprised to find that the different selling environments send different selling signals to you. Pick up on what they're saying, and you'll be happy you did!

Manage Your Tones to Seem Sincere

Another nonverbal dimension of selling is one that isn't discussed very much, in part, because it isn't strictly nonverbal: our tone of voice. But it can have a tremendous impact upon our sales results, so we should pay considerable attention to it.

Case in Point: The Voice Mail Lady

Have you noticed that there is one person who is recording many of the voice mail announcements right now for major companies? She seems to do each one in exactly the same tonal way.

The calls start with the text: "Thank you for calling" and the name of the company is mentioned. If you listen carefully, you'll notice her pitch moves up, pointedly, on the word calling. This is at variance with how the word is normally delivered, which is with a flat tone.

Does she know something that many people don't know about the connection between tone and customer response? With regard to pitch, the answer is yes.

When we orchestrate our tones to support our words we're regarded as being sincere. Unfortunately, many of the most professional sales organizations default in managing tone. Naturals, however, pay close attention to this crucial dimension of communication.

When our tone collides with our text, guess which one wins in getting its message through to the listener?

Tone.

Sarcasm is a classic example. When someone says the words, "Well, that's great," we have to monitor the tone to determine if he's on the level.

If he sings the words so they move upward in pitch, we'll believe he means what the words say. If, on the other hand, his tone stair steps downward, we'll know to take the opposite of what his words are saying to be true.

Many sellers sound inadvertently sarcastic. Note how they say the first words of their inbound call script: "How may I help you?" "Help" almost always moves up in tone, but "you" moves down.

This sends a tonal signal that says, "I really don't want to help—I'm just going through the motions." If the same rep is taught to make the "you" reach the highest pitch level of any word in the phrase, she'll almost always sound more sincere and more willing to help.

Here's the rub. Most non-naturals who are using their intuition will formulate a tonal pattern that sounds insincere. To make consistently high sales, we need to analyze our messages for tonal nuances and then deliberately assign the right tones to our text.

When we do, our customers will sing our praises because we're singing our phrases!

Posture Counts!

Confident salespeople carry themselves well. They square their shoulders and pull in their chins. By doing so, they give themselves an aura of authority.

Case in Point: Physical Presence

Rick is a twenty-five-year veteran of pharmaceutical sales. He stands about 6 feet 6 inches and weighs over 250 pounds. He has been a self-made, multi-millionaire for years, and he enjoys a number of big homes, fancy cars, and country club memberships.

To what ability does he attribute his earning power and sales results? He declares:

"I intimidate doctors by standing right over them. I'm big and they're small, and they sign on the dotted line when I hand them my pen. There's simply nothing else to it," he claims.

You don't have to be tall to SEEM larger and in command. If you use the right posture, you'll appear to be more powerful and help yourself to more sales.

Smell Sells!

In a bygone era, men who wore after-shave lotion or cologne were considered unusual. This has changed over the years partly due to brilliant marketing on the part of cosmetics manufacturers and retailers.

Obviously, modern men and women believe that it makes a good impression if they smell pleasant. If you decide to wear scented products, please make sure to invest in upscale ones that aren't cheap or audacious. Try to apply them in moderation, so they are subtle.

The same principle applies to maintaining fresh breath. I'd avoid chewing gum in a prospect's presence unless you're a ballplayer who is talking to a major league scout.

Small breath mints are perfect, and they will make your presentations less distracting!

This chapter has shown you how important nonverbal communication is to selling. In Chapter 6, you'll learn how naturals multiply their effectiveness by using different sales media and strategies. These include networking, letters, faxes, e-mail, phone calls, personal visits, product guarantees, computers, and the Internet.

You'll see how naturals succeed by vowing to never waste their time in the next chapter!

NEVER
EVER
WASTE
YOUR TIME!

One of the most critical skills you can learn from naturally talented salespeople is how to determine the quality and buying intentions of prospects. You'll also need to learn to exploit several sales media: networking, letters, faxes, e-mail, phone calls, personal visits, computer software, and the Internet.

Today's natural born salespeople aren't narrow specialists who limit themselves to using only a single sales medium. They can't afford to be because their competitors are learning to exploit a number of media to extend their reach and effectiveness.

Naturals can't rely exclusively upon the gift of gab or upon pressing the flesh in an ever accelerating global marketplace. They need to be equally adept at utilizing alternative and new media to augment their arsenal of competitive weapons.

We're going to examine some of the most effective tools that are at your disposal, and I'll show you how naturals are using their superior instincts to squeeze the most from them.

Ten Prospects to Avoid

How valuable would it be if you could know in advance what customers were going to be a big pain in the you know what?

Would you avoid them and just concentrate on closing the better ones? This is exactly what I try to do, and I can tell you it has made me a much better salesperson and one happy camper!

How can you tell who will become a bad versus a good customer?

Let's look at how you can use a natural's instincts and judgment to save time and cut to the chase. The trick is to recognize certain characteristics of the lousy buyer early in the sales process. There are ten characteristics of people who you shouldn't sell—who simply aren't worth your valuable time or your attention. If you avoid them, you'll also preserve your priceless positive attitude.

1. *Turtles.* These are slow decision-makers, or people who have no timetable for completing a purchase. They have no perceived urgency and nothing you can do can make them disclose or accelerate their timetable. Don't waste your time with turtles and you'll have more time to concentrate on catching the hares.

2. *Control Freaks.* These are people who won't let you do your presentation. They're people who won't play the game. If you ask them a question, they will avoid giving you an answer. If you make a declarative statement, they will contradict you. Control freaks feel the need to dominate. Avoid them or you'll only end up talking in circles.

3. *Deceivers.* These are people who don't tell you the whole truth. They fail to disclose vital information that can cause major problems after the initial sale. It's imperative to have an honest relationship with your client. If you feel vital information is deliberately withheld from you, abandon the project immediately to avoid any further deception. This way you can concentrate on meaningful relationships.

4. *Gangs.* Whenever more than three people are in a room expecting you to make a sales presentation, you're probably facing the equivalent of a firing squad. It's very hard to have a meaningful give-and-take session with more than two or three people at a time. Whenever possible, try to identify an enthusiastic buyer who will champion your product or services within his company and break down the opposition into bite-sized groups.

5. *Paranoids.* These are people who tell you that they've been burned before. All they tend to do is refer to negative past experiences. If these are the people you are encountering, their perception will become reality for them. More often then not, what they'll do is project their negative expectations on to you and your firm. Even if you're faultless in your performance, they'll see demons where none exist and cause you a lot of trouble.

6. *Jacks.* These are arrogant souls who claim to be jacks of all trades. After hearing a few of your ideas, they'll suddenly become expert in your field and pretend they don't need you. Be careful with them because they like to swipe ideas, repackage them, and pass them off as originals.

7. *Hiders.* These are people who might strike up a buying scenario and just as quickly turn and hide from you. Inexplicably, they'll refuse to take your calls and won't call you back if you leave messages. Best tactic: don't throw good time after bad by chasing them.

8. *Antagonists.* These people like to argue and put you through your paces. They think salespeople are overpaid and underworked. Secretly, they're jealous of you and don't want you to be successful. They'll probe to find out what kind of car you drive and other details about your affluent lifestyle. Don't waste your time.

9. *Insolvents.* These people simply don't have the financial ability to buy. Nonetheless, they enjoy kicking tires and being treated as if they're important. They'll waste as much of your time as you're willing to give them. It's tempting to go along with them because they're easy to talk to and they're nice.

10. *Negotiators.* These people make everything sound like it's a commodity, even high quality services. They're determined to shrink your margins and kill profits. They know the price of everything and the value of nothing. You'll identify them easily because they come to you armed with all of the names of your competitors and they'll announce fictitious bids that they've extracted from your adversaries. Avoid them.

Keep these ten tips in mind. You'll avoid the losers and invest your precious time with winners.

Can You Send Me Some Literature?

How can you tell who is a real prospect versus someone who is just requesting literature? At first, they seem strikingly alike.

For instance, they might call you after visiting your web site or your booth at a trade show and ask for some literature.

We shouldn't automatically say sure and pop something into the mail. First, we should probe to determine whether they have a real need. Otherwise, we can end up wasting a lot of our time and precious resources on folks who have no serious interest in buying.

Case in Point: Low Potential Prospects

The other day I received a call from a fellow consultant who had heard that I had some intriguing methods. I don't hear that word very often, because most serious people don't use it when they're shopping for sales, service, or technical support training. They might say effective methods, or useful, or even advanced, but not intriguing.

Intriguing is a leisure term, an adjective we use to describe the novel that we've momentarily put down as we retrieve our umbrella drink. It isn't a serious buying word. So that fellow gets no literature!

Likewise, the woman who called and left a voice mail that said she was curious about what we did, and could I send her some information, please? Not no, but HECK NO!

I'm in business to satisfy real needs and not to indulge fleeting, casual curiosities. Again, if callers won't tell me they have an immediate buying interest, I have no time for them, and I suggest you follow this example.

But what happens when prospects don't want to reveal their true needs or intentions? What if they ask for literature, but they won't express a serious interest in buying anything? What should we do, then?

Yesterday, I received an inquiry from someone who was like this. She had heard about my training classes from another seminar company and she wanted to obtain a copy of our schedule.

What I found fascinating about our conversation was the degree of secrecy that she tried to inject into it. Instead of responding frankly and openly to my questions about her specific needs, she insisted that we speak about superficialities.

I got the feeling that she could have been a spy or a foil for someone who was doing some competitive benchmarking. Within a few minutes I established that she wasn't going to purchase a specific product, but she asked to be sent information anyway.

I've estimated that sellers waste at least one follow-up hour chasing people who have requested literature yet have zero buying intent.

Of course, there's always the remote possibility that people will purchase something at a future date because we were responsive to their first request.

The natural's view is that we shouldn't cultivate admitted nonbuyers. Someone who refuses to disclose his real needs is treated as a nonbuyer.

I am willing to make a minor accommodation. If a prospect has e-mail, I'll generally transmit a standard description of one of our products. It takes about thirty seconds and it's nearly free. I'll hesitate to send a fax because it involves phone costs and labor. It is very unlikely that I'll assemble and mail a package, which is the costliest response.

If you're using a needs-based, consultative method of selling, you should be wary of wasting time with people who disqualify themselves from receiving further attention. Marshal all of your resources to deal with people who state real, present needs that you can satisfy at a profit.

You'll find you have liberated more than enough time to get close to the prospects who really deserve your time and your attention.

Faxing Beats Mailing in More Ways than One

The fax machine can be an extremely powerful and efficient selling tool when it's used properly. Using it in nontraditional situations can pay off, bigtime, as this case points out.

Case in Point: Which Sells Better—An Ugly Fax or a Beautiful Brochure?

When I used to line up sponsors for my seminars, I'd follow a three step selling procedure: (1) I'd make a cold call by phone; (2) I'd mail a small packet of information along with a note that memorialized the understanding we reached during the call; and (3) I'd follow up about a week later by phone to confirm the deal.

Pretty standard process, and it would get good results for me. The greatest delay, of course, was (2), the delivery of the mail. That would take two–three days, and it would mean, invariably, that even if you called someone on Monday, you couldn't really follow up your mailer until the following Monday.

The fax machine has changed this process radically. Not only is your written material received, potentially, within seconds, but you've inaugurated a buying tempo that is much faster than ever before. The very speed of your outbound fax tends to lend urgency to the deliberations of your prospects.

Instead of feeling that they can take up to a week to pore over mailed material, they sense, after receiving a fax, that you're going to probably follow up within no more than a day or two. So their net amount of decision time has been compressed up to six days because of the fax machine.

Are there times when it is better to send documents?

Clearly, if your firm requires an original signed contract then that's the way to go.

What about the look of the materials you want to convey? Will your company and your offer look better by mail than by fax?

Sometimes, but not always. In a recent jewelry sales campaign, we found that a phone call followed by a fax was more effective in generating sales than a call followed by a mailer that contained clearer photos of the jewelry items. You would expect that better photo resolution would be more persuasive in selling jewelry, but it was less persuasive.

I believe buyers make allowances for faxed transmittals that they won't make for mailed materials. One expects a photo to be pretty, perhaps even artistic, while a fax is expected to look fuzzy.

Recipients of mailers are simply more critical of appearances than are those who get faxes.

The verbal persuasion contained in your original phone call takes on more importance for the fax buyer. If you made a solid phone presentation, the fax will help you. It enables a positively predisposed prospect to justify making a fast go decision.

It also keeps the sales process simple. Add details through elaborate visuals and you might be inadvertently introducing complications that can delay or derail the buying process.

Offering to fax someone information can also qualify or disqualify buyers. In most cases, if a prospect rejects your offer to receive a fax and insists that you just mail it, they're losers. They don't feel any urgency to buy, and they're telling you not to tie up their fax machine with offers in which they have no interest.

Instead of having to wait for a week or more to discover whether you have a good prospect, the offer of a fax can spare you a wasted cycle of transmission and follow-up activity.

You can get more and faster sales with a fax machine, but you also might realize greater efficiencies in the qualification and persuasion process. And your brochures and other visuals could be more effective by fax than in person.

When Should You Substitute Sales Media?

When I first got e-mail, I was like a little kid with a brand new plastic hammer:

Everyone started looking like a nail to me, so I hammered them all with my new toy.

I even e-mailed to prospects who specifically asked to be faxed, mailed, or phoned. Why was I so chauvinistic about wanting to use e-mail?

It's fast, cheap, and saves paper and trees! These are good rationales, right? But what I wasn't tuning into were the signals from some of my prospects that said *We don't LIKE e-mail!*

Or, more commonly, they didn't know how to work their e-mail programs, so they gave me bad addresses. My messages would then go around the world and return to me as undeliverable.

I'd have to call them back and send them a fax, which is often what they wanted all along! It takes a good amount of sensitivity to determine which medium to use with certain prospects, and this isn't always easy to know, even if you ask them.

Some prospects aren't really urgently interested in retaining my consulting services if they request literature be sent by mail instead of being faxed. Think about this request for a moment.

If you really need to make change happen in your organization, can you go about it at a leisurely snail-mail pace? No way! You're going to opt for speed. The same folks who ask for a brochure by mail will also couch their request in some conspicuous language, which should be a tip off that they're not real buyers.

Use Sales Software to Track Your Customers

I strongly urge you to use sales software to keep track of your customers' interests, purchases, and comments. It may be the best way I have ever found of getting and staying organized.

But now that I've said this, there is a downside to using databases that should be cautioned about. Although it can help you get you organized, beware of falling into the clerical trap.

When you think of a salesperson, what characteristics come to mind? Glib, personable, and aggressive are a few adjectives that might fit.

What about organized? Not really. Salespeople aren't generally high on the idea of filling in a lot of paper work, dotting the i's, and crossing the t's. They tend to be big picture instead of detail people. When they joined the working world they didn't labor over the question of whether they should go into bookkeeping or into sales.

It is their lack of organizational prowess that makes them attractive candidates for lead tracking software. This product helps salespeople to capture basic information about prospects and set up certain recall dates for staying in touch with them.

It can be handy and effective, but it can easily sidetrack salespeople into wasting their time and energy with prospects who aren't worth pursuing. Here's what I mean.

Let's say you are given a new software package. The first thing you do is load it with a lot of suspects, or people who you think are worth contacting. The number may easily run into the thousands, if only because this is the denomination through which database vendors sell their lists.

So you have a good PC and thousands of people to call. You start your calls and, inevitably, the great majority result in no's, stalls, and changed names and phone numbers. Naturally, you're going to want to input this information into your new database.

This takes lots of clerical time—time that you could be investing in other calls. One of the painful insights you may have is that you're gilding a wilted lily. If you merely had a suspect to begin with, why go to such lengths documenting changes in its status? Isn't this a supreme waste of time?

Here's a related problem. You contact someone who requests literature. You misinterpret this as an expression of deep interest. You mail it. You enter this information into the database. Three or four days later you call the person. You get voice mail or learn she's away from the office. Your database asks you when you want to call again? You input the next day.

Same result, so what's next? If you're like most people, you'll feel you have a great investment in the person as you scan your electronically preserved history with the account.

You won't want to throw in the towel and delete the person from your database because you've been oversold on the value of finding and keeping prospect names. So you add them to your mailing list and repeat the same procedure to no avail.

It has been said that there are two kinds of prospects: cherries and pits. Cherries have a lot of promise and we should be looking for them when we prospect. Pits aren't cherries. They consume your time and prevent you from finding cherries.

The problem with lead tracking software is it discourages us from calling a pit a pit. It implores us to treat pits as we would cherries, and this is a tremendously wasteful endeavor.

Tracking every last detail about people who don't matter isn't a virtue. Salespeople should not allow a machine to intrude upon the process of judging the value of various suspects and prospects.

Natural born salespeople know in their gut when there is a prospect worth pursuing. They also appreciate that many of them aren't worth an additional second of their time, and they rightfully jettison the pits into oblivion.

So by all means use sales software, but make it your servant instead of your master.

A Smart Way to Use the Internet

I realize that you may feel desensitized to the whole idea of involving the Internet in your selling processes because there has been so much hype in promoting it. But there is at least one way that I urge you to exploit it:

Use the Internet as a quick and cheap literature fulfillment medium.

By having some basic information about your company or yourself on the Web, you'll find you can save a lot of money on sending out brochures, tracking them, and paying your clerical assistants.

Once people have visited your site you can have another conversation with them to see if they're qualified to buy. If so, then take the relationship to the next step.

Don't Forget the Human Touch

I've covered a number of media in this chapter, and it would be easy to infer that I think these are superior to meeting with people face to face, but I don't. Personal visits are extremely helpful, especially where you're selling so-called intangibles.

Case in Point: Personal Contact

One of my clients is a six figure salesperson for a small mutual fund company. He spends about two weeks out of every month on planes and in hotels visiting his client base.

Would he love to spend more time with his wife and seven-year-old daughter? You bet! But he can't.

His clients will stop buying from his firm if he becomes merely a virtual presence. In our era of no-load funds and increasing financial sophistication, his buyers could easily cut his company out of the food chain if they wished.

He knows the best way to preserve their business is by preserving his relationships with them. And there's nothing quite like being there to assure this happens.

Networking: An Updated Medium of Prospecting

In an earlier chapter, I mentioned that the way I broke into the leasing business was by making cold calls over the phone. This is still the way many new sellers cut their teeth in a number of industries, especially in financial companies.

But it also has drawbacks. It's not always an efficient sales medium from a time management standpoint. Sometimes, you have to make tons of calls to find just a few nuggets of opportunity.

Part of the inefficiency is attributable to the fact that there aren't enough GREAT lists from which to make calls. By great, I mean lists that: (1) have a sufficient number of names and phone numbers to keep you busy; (2) contain a large proportion of highly qualified and positively predisposed prospects; and (3) are easily obtained through commercial sources.

In actual fact, LOUSY lists are abundant. Just phone any major list company and they'll offer the same generic lists that are available everywhere, even on the Internet at no cost!

What naturals do to improve the odds and enhance their lists is NETWORK to find suitable buyers.

How do they do this? They may begin their day by calling someone from a poor list, but they don't delude themselves into believing that this individual is a buyer. They USE THE FIRST CONTACT TO HELP THEM FIND GREAT PROSPECTS.

In fact, they might begin a conversation with the words, "I realize that you might not be exactly the person I need to speak to, but perhaps you could help me to identify who he or she may be, and I'd really be grateful for that..."

Case in Point: Networking in Hollywood

I've already mentioned that my dad was a real natural. What I didn't tell you is the fact that he was a superb networker as well.

When I was just seventeen, he showed me how to network my way into the entertainment industry. I was an aspiring actor with a number of theater roles to my credit, and I felt it was time to break into movies and the bigtime.

Dad, a consummate phone person, sat me down and said, "Watch me, son. I'm going to get you an agent."

I think I laughed out of a combination of insecurity and excitement. He knew he was putting me on the spot as well as into the spotlight. He looked into my eyes as if to ask *Are you really ready for this?*

I wiped the goofy grin off my face and took a seat beside him on the sofa. I asked him, "Are you actually going to call a talent agency?"

"Nope," he replied with an impish grin. "I'm going to do better than that. I'm going to call the people who HIRE talent agents and their clients."

I was confused, but intrigued. "Who's that?" I asked.

"What's the biggest studio you can think of, Gary, that's also in the neighborhood?"

"Fox?" I responded.

"Yep," he said. "Let's call the Casting Director at Fox and find out who his or her FAVORITE agent is, shall we?"

He got directory assistance for Fox's number, and, miraculously, within a few minutes he was speaking to a Casting Director. Just seconds after that, he emerged with the name of a well known talent agent.

I was stunned. Not only was he networking, but he was using a lot of savvy to determine with whom to network first so he would develop leverage in a later call.

But Dad wasn't through. Immediately, without as much as a one second pause, he phoned the agent. After quickly introducing himself he said:

"My son thinks he has what it takes to be a successful actor, and so-and-so at Fox recommended you as being the best person for making that dream come true."

After a little small talk, my Dad had set an appointment for me for the following week. In that meeting, I sold the agent on representing me.

Five Good Reasons to Add Networking to Your Toolkit

Why should we network when we can buy people's business through other less intimate means, such as marketing, conventional selling, and advertising? We should network for these reasons.

1. *It doesn't take a lot of money, and anyone can do it.* How much did it cost my Dad to line up the agent? Two local phone calls and a few minutes of his time.

2. *It's fast and surprisingly direct.* We can target who we need to contact with precision and get their attention in a fraction of the time it takes to develop a shotgun style ad campaign.

3. *It's friendly.* There's a social component to networking that is rewarding in itself. It's fun to make friends while we extend our spheres of influence.

4. *It brings us hidden opportunities, lucky breaks, and other treasures that we would never hear about through official channels.*

5. *Networking is a basic human activity.* When our ancient ancestors were sitting around their caves and someone approached, what was the first question they probably asked themselves? *Do I know this person?* Then, they'd turn to each other, and ask: *Do you know him?* Unless the visitor could quickly establish that he knew someone they knew, he was pounced on or chased away.

Not much has evolved since that time long, long ago. We're still territorial, even if our turf has grown to include cyberspace. We are willing to share our business and personal resources, first and foremost, with people we know and then with people who come highly recommended to us. Become one of those recommended people and you will make the most of your precious sales time.

Make Your Phone Calls and Letters More Effective

Too many salespeople see phone calls and sales letters as secondary tools in their success arsenal. But used properly, they'll save you time and bolster your face-to-face selling efforts.

Most salespeople meet their downfalls at the hands of mere secretaries and assistants. Instead of spending the majority of their phone hours speaking to real buyers, sellers are shot down by gate-keepers who see it as a personal challenge to prevent us from speaking to their bosses.

I'm going to provide your with some vital information that will enable you to get through secretarial screening twice as often. This will turbocharge your efforts, and you'll find yourself spending much more time with people who really matter: decision makers.

Screeners are scripted. They almost always ask, "Who's calling?" and "May I tell him what this is about?" But if you begin your phone call in a different way, it'll throw them completely off.

Instead of ASKING if you can speak to Bill, try saying this:

Hello, Gary Goodman, Goodman Communications, for Bill please, thank you.

They'll be so taken aback that they don't have to grill you to find out who you are, that they'll often put you through right away.

This works for several reasons. First, you'll throw them off of their scripts. Second, you'll sound confident and upfront with them. And most important, you'll sound polite, professional, and firm.

You'll sound like you deserve to speak with Bill. There are several other lines that I've crafted for conquering screening. If you're interested in refining your phone techniques, I suggest you take a look at my recent book, *Telemarketing For Non-Telemarketers*, published by Dartnell.

Tips for Making Your Letters Sparkle

The best sales letters are really a lot like very concise sales presentations. Here are a few tips for making your letters as effective as they can be:

1. *Shorter letters are read thoroughly, and longer ones aren't.* If I'm writing a cover letter and sending it with some testimonials, I'll usually keep its length down to one page.

There is an important exception. If your letter is designed to complete the sale and it asks for a person to purchase the product or to make the ultimate buying commitment, then take as much space as you need to tell your story.

Example: The Detailed Sales Letter

When I am doing a mailing to fill my seminars with paying participants, I design my letters so they ask the reader to commit to registering right away. So I may compose a letter that consists of four or five single spaced pages.

Assume that you're writing for folks who ARE interested. These individuals CRAVE DETAILS, so it pays to provide them.

2. *Try using the PEP formula described in an earlier chapter.* It is not only a great improvisational tool, but its three-part structure is especially ideal for organizing short letters.

3. *Make sure your first line or headline is a grabber.* If you can tap into a need right away through a question, you're on the right track.

Example: Powerful Headlines

When I'm promoting one of my telemarketing seminars, I'll use this question as my headline:

Is telemarketing turnover killing your profitability?

I go on to discuss how the average telemarketing department experiences over 200 percent annual employee turnover and what this means in terms of ushering in higher costs and lower sales.

The key to a great headline is that it makes the reader want to learn more about your company and your offer. If you can put them into this mood, it's highly likely they'll read to the bottom of the page.

Close Deals Faster with Guarantees

One of the best ways to save time and multiply sales is by offering product or service guarantees. I know from plenty of experience that they get prospects to make buying decisions in record time, if only because they believe their bad decisions can be reversed, or, at least corrected.

Guarantees are becoming a way of life in sales and marketing. Everywhere you turn there seems to be one. Recently, a seminar company offered a lifetime guarantee, if you can believe it.

It said, "If you ever come to feel that this course wasn't wonderful, we'll give you your money back!" Imagine ninety years from now waking from your all-day nap to discover that the French cooking class you took nearly a century before let you down.

Never could master that darned souffle! Why not get a refund? Even McDonald's, the icon of value, has used guarantees to tout its burgers and new menu items.

Guarantees can build sales very quickly because they can cut through the chaff of the most resistant prospects. They can also get customers to spend more than they anticipated.

I suggest you use a guarantee in these situations.

1. *You're the new kid on the block.*

Let's say you're just starting out and having to fight entrenched competitors. How do you get people to try you out? By taking the financial risk out of it, and this is what a guarantee accomplishes. Hampton Inns took the lead in this area a few years ago by offering a money back guarantee for the first night's stay if the lodger found it unsatisfactory. This was a way to earn major attention for a new national chain while asserting a quality pledge that differentiated Hampton from its many competitors.

2. *There's been negative publicity or bad word of mouth about your product or company.*

This will reassure people who are interested in buying from you but who are concerned. The Jaguar automobile division of Ford Motor Company did this effectively.

I've never met anyone who isn't impressed with the looks of a classic Jaguar. But, as *The Wall Street Journal* has reported, owners often have mechanical nightmares with it.

A few years ago, Jaguar responded by offering the public a thirty-day, free test drive. Other car companies, like Audi, have gone further by offering full maintenance contracts along with their cars. These promotions don't last long. They seem to be short-term expedients for restoring a sense of confidence. After they've succeeded, they're usually set aside.

3. *When your product or service is a true innovation.*

One of my clients is the fellow who sold the Berlin Wall, one tiny piece at a time. Remember those little rocks glued onto plaques a few years ago in department stores? His idea. He sold a million of them in six months. They came with certificates of authenticity. Another name for guarantees.

4. *Your product or service changes buying habits.*

The same client who sold the Berlin Wall came to me with a new product he wanted to market that purifies water one drop at a time through a hand held, pen-like dispenser. He asked me my opinion, and I told him it would only be marketable with an unconditional guarantee because folks weren't used to buying pure water that way. They're used to bottles and filters.

Federal Express, when it invented overnight delivery service with its 10:00 A.M. overnight delivery guarantee, is another example of an innovator having to use a guarantee. Could you sell Christmas trees, puppies, or kitties by phone or through mail order? Probably not without a guarantee, because you're changing important buying rituals and sentimental traditions.

5. *When you're selling by phone or mail to sell sensory products that usually appeal to a prospect's taste, touch, or vision.*

Fine art and vintage wines come to mind. A guarantee might substitute for someone proving to herself with her own senses the value of your offer. If you want to substitute telemarketers for field salespeople, you might have to arm your phone people with guarantees as well.

6. *When you're trying to win back lost customers.*

After all, why should they risk disappointment or failure with you again? Bankrupt airlines attempting to return to normal service will dabble with satisfaction guarantees for this reason.

7. *When the risk of loss is high, or when a product's potential defects are not subject to inspection.*

Big ticket items call for guarantees. That's why most cars, houses, and computers are sold with warranties

8. *When your profit margins are high. Your additional sales will more than compensate for your losses from returns.*

9. *Only when your company culture will tolerate returns and their demands.*

Some companies are too egotistical or temperamental to accept product returns. One of my clients owns photography studios across the country. They offer a guarantee, but they're utterly miffed if you exercise it and they show their contempt openly.

They hire people who believe they are part of the high fashion industry, and their haughtiness is very thinly disguised. My suggestion to them: either make it easy to utilize the guarantee or stop offering it altogether. Other firms, like Nordstrom, have built dynasties upon unconditional and often wildly generous guarantees. And their patrons truly seem to appreciate them.

10. *To sell services only when there are stop losses available.*

Use guarantees to sell personal services only when you can stop your losses before completing the entire service. If you're a C.P.A., work up the numbers but don't fill out the tax return before getting client approval.

If you're a barber, stop after cutting the left side of the head. Just kidding. You can see why service guarantees have problems.

Guarantees will certainly earn you additional sales. They'll also have an interesting impact upon how you do business. When you strongly assert a quality guarantee, you have to build your product or service so it lives up to buyer expectations.

This imposes a quality frame of mind upon your firm. Suddenly, you have a challenging standard to live up to. But achieving a higher level of satisfaction will win repeat sales for you as well as higher profits for your company.

Know Yourself and You'll Save Lots of Time and Energy

In an earlier section of this book, I mentioned that it doesn't make sense for sellers to press or try to force sales to happen. When we do this, we usually choke.

In the same vein, it makes sense to ask yourself, "Am I in the right sales job for me, given my temperament?" One way to make this determination is by evaluating the compensation plan that you're operating under.

Your success or failure in a job may be based upon whether there is a good fit between your reinforcement needs and the reinforcement schedule through which you're being paid.

Are you cut out to be a straight commission seller, or would you feel more comfortable and actually produce more if you were paid a flat salary? You should do some soul searching to figure out exactly what sort of pay plan and benefits package will turn you on or off.

Personally, I like a straight pay for performance situation. If I produce, I eat. And if I don't produce, I move on.

This is how I've been managing for over seventeen years as an independent consultant. Either I put business on the books, or I'm in trouble.

You may be less risk tolerant and operate better under a scheme where you get some sort of pay, come what may. This could mean a draw against commissions or a salary plus commissions. No matter how you're paid, there is an important psychological principle that you should bear in mind:

The schedule upon which we receive our rewards is as important, if not more important, than the amount of the rewards themselves.

Take your typical commission salesperson. She probably earns money through spurts of achievement. One month she'll reach the pinnacle of success, and in the next she may be cast into a valley of despair.

To survive as a commission salesperson, you have to be able to tolerate, and perhaps even enjoy, these peaks and valleys. Most Americans would find such swings in earnings and perceived success as intolerable. Even if the commission person earns more at the end of the year, there is greater satisfaction in steady paychecks for most salaried people.

As you can imagine, it's vital to understand what your preferences are so you don't end up in the wrong compensation plan for your temperament. You should also be aware of how your reinforcement schedule preference is limiting or potentially depressing your earnings.

Case in Point: Six and Seven Figure Salespeople

I've had the privilege of being a consultant to what might be called, the sales elite. These are people who earn $250,000 and up in commissions during a single year. You can see the true impact of reinforcement schedules by observing these hardy souls.

Take Don, an institutional bond salesman. On a single sale a few months ago, he earned a commission in excess of ONE MILLION DOLLARS. This result came from a deal that closed in November.

From January through October of that year, he completely struck out. No earnings. No paychecks. The year was nearly 85 percent over with by the time he earned his first sale.

He went from feeling like a bum to being king of the hill overnight. The pain he suffered to his ego, self-esteem, and bank account for over ten months, however, left some scar tissue.

He was definitely humbled by his prolonged slump. You might be thinking that he can buy a lot of therapy with his million bucks, and you're right. He can afford to recuperate, take a vacation, and rebuild his regard for himself as a professional.

He knows all of this and realizes that the really big bucks are reserved for the people who can handle the excruciating pain of uncertainty that comes with being a commission-only salesperson.

If you look at Don's selling skills and at his techniques, he doesn't differ very much from an average salaried seller.

What sets him apart is the fact that he has developed unusually high frustration tolerance, which enables him to weather storms that would batter others to pieces.

Would you like to earn more? Consider controlling your reinforcement schedule instead of having it unconsciously control you. Find or create a compensation agreement that fits you and that's workable for your employer.

You'll definitely find it's worth your time and energy.

This chapter has shown you how to make the most of your time and the sales tools that are available. In our final chapter, we're going to explore how you can conquer your slumps, setbacks, and career comas to stay on top where you belong!

CHAPTER 7

TRANSFORM EVERY SETBACK, REJECTION, AND SLUMP INTO A MAJOR ADVANTAGE

We all experience slumps. Some days we're on top of the world, and the next we feel we're moving inexorably into deeper and deeper levels of misery. Let's look at how and why slumps happen and what you can do to work your way out of one.

Slumps happen to average folks, as well as to high achievers in any walk of life. They even plague the rich and famous.

Winston Churchill, Great Britain's Prime Minister during World War II, used to suffer from what he termed "the Black Dog." It was a severe visitation of self-doubt and depression. When he was in that state, he was emotionally paralyzed. Nothing he did seemed to work.

But he'd pull himself from these depths to rise to major occasions. He always seemed to rescue himself from the thorns of dourness.

We can all bounce back from slumps with renewed vigor and a stronger and better sense of ourselves if we fully understand them. And I hope this chapter will help you to make yours shorter, less intense, and ultimately, much more productive.

Turning Lemons into Lemonade

Natural born salespeople have an uncanny ability to turn lemons into lemonade and waste into treasure. They accomplish this mighty feat, day in and day out, by controlling their attitudes and behavior.

It isn't as if naturals don't fall into funks or experience setbacks and rejections. They do, believe me. But they learn from them while making the down times and the reversals pay them back.

Even kings have slumps, but as the true story that follows will show, they come back from them stronger than ever before.

The Two Kings

When it came to selling, my Dad, as you know, was a true natural. Congenial, well spoken, and low-key, he could communicate deftly with anyone. If he had been a singer, he would have sounded like Sinatra.

When I was still in college, I watched him go through one of the most difficult slumps of his life. It was as if his career had suddenly succumbed to a coma.

Among other things, he sold advertising. For years, at various firms, he was the number one salesman. No one could touch him. Then, he changed companies, and, for what seemed to be the longest time, he simply couldn't close a deal.

Weeks and months passed, and no one said yes. He was more than perplexed. His strike-out streak was so bad that it could have easily turned into an existential crisis. That's when you doubt your abilities, the quality of your product, and even your proper place in the universe.

It hurt as I watched the humbling of a sales king who, less than a year before, could walk into any advertising firm in the country and write his own ticket. Fortunately, Dad's boss, a fellow by the name of Mac Strauss, kept the faith. He appreciated that sooner or later Dad would roar back like a lion.

Elvis Meets Dad

All slumps end. Ironically, in my Dad's case, it took another King who was slumping and needed a comeback to help my Dad to make his return to sales greatness.

The person who helped Dad snap his losing streak was none other than Elvis Presley. Dad's comeback deal was a huge package of advertising that Colonel Parker bought.

The Colonel managed Elvis' career and was the genius behind the engineering of a live stage show for Elvis at the Las Vegas Hilton. That show would put Elvis back on top of the rock and roll world after a long bout with relative obscurity.

After that sale, my father never had reason to doubt his abilities again. He quickly soared to the number one spot at his company, and that's where he remained: on top.

I have often wondered what it took, psychologically, for my Dad to persevere as long as he did in the face of unrelenting rejection. What did he tell himself to enable him to carry on during those difficult times?

Here are some of the tips he would have passed on to us for sticking it out through the worst of selling slumps:

1. *Remember your successes.* You've succeeded before, and you will succeed again. Summon to mind the feeling that success is imminent, and this will give you an aura of confidence and assurance, which is attractive to buyers.

Give yourself minor successes along the way that you can celebrate. Break down success into smaller units such as the number of prospects telephoned, visited, and followed-up. Each advancement in the buying process can be seen as an achievement that you can feel good about.

2. *Take a lesson from statistics.* Events can distribute themselves in peculiar ways that may be disconnected from any apparent

single cause. You could be trying as hard as ever, yet your efforts still don't get results.

If we flipped a coin one hundred times, we could predict that it would land face up about 50 percent of the time and face down 50 percent of the time. If you do this, you may find that your particular series of flips results in a 60-40, a 70-30, or an 80-20 distribution. Perhaps one of several million times a series of 100 flips will yield 100 heads and zero tails.

Translated into street talk, sometimes when you're hot, you're hot; when you're not, you're not.

3. *Your slump may NOT be the result of your attitude, techniques, or ability.* In the flipping illustration, do you think the skill with which you tossed the coins in the air would determine the outcomes? If you held the coin differently or put a forward or backward spin on it, would it be any more likely to come up heads or tails? No.

4. *Your slump could begin to affect your attitudes, techniques, and ability if you aren't careful.* A seemingly random run of negative outcomes or nonsales could start to be fueled by you, thus elongating your slump. If you opened a series of five doors, and after each one you had a pie thrown into your face, what would you do upon opening the sixth?

You'd duck! Ducking, in sales terms, means looking and sounding like a loser who doesn't expect to sell, and who a client would be afraid to reward with a purchase. Stand tall, and you'll outlast the pies.

Three Quick Fixes for Ending Slumps

When I get the feeling that I'm losing upward momentum and that I'm starting to descend into a pit, there are three quick fixes that I consider using to defeat the gloom.

1. *Do nothing, and I mean NOTHING.*
2. *Do minor, brainless work that keeps my hands busy.*
3. *Try entirely new tactics.*

Let's look at these options in some detail.

My First Great Tip: Do Nothing!

The first approach is consistent with the idea of doing no harm. Once you realize you're in a funk, that's a breakthrough in itself. That insight can preclude you from doing rash things.

For example, when I'm not 100 percent emotionally, I want to force good things to happen. I might feel like calling sluggish prospects and using a rush-rush message to get them off the fence.

Almost always, this kind of pressure backfires. If there was any buying interest, that's a good way to squelch it.

Instead of ignoring your slump, appreciate that you're in one. Option number one then is to resolve to not make things worse.

You might choose to take a mental health day off. A twenty-five minute drive to the ocean works wonders for me. I find I'm in a completely different environment—one in which vacationers are enjoying themselves. Moreover, I see people driving new cars and spending bundles of money. This is really critical to snapping me out of my gloom. How come?

It reminds me that there are millions of other people who are succeeding, BIGTIME, at the precise moment that I feel I'm failing!

This thought might make some people feel worse, but it makes me feel a whole heck of a lot better. It says:

If they're doing it, so can I!

Rod Carew, the Angels' hitting coach and baseball Hall of Fame member, has a theory about batters who are slumping. "Usually," Carew says, "the reason is mental." It doesn't have to do with the slumper's physical mechanics.

So when I'm at the beach, I buy a gourmet coffee and watch the parade of affluence and easy-does-it living float by. Believe me, it's tremendously calming. It's my way of not doing in a fun, rejuvenating manner.

But if your style is different, you might choose to sleep in, or if you report to work, try to shut your door if you have one.

If you're really moody, I'd delay making major decisions—at least, temporarily. For instance, at any given time, I have to negotiate contracts with hotels in order to offer my seminars on a national basis. It's a sales task despite the fact that I'm paying them.

I have to sell them on giving me a great conference room at a discounted rate and to hold the date(s) of my programs without requiring immediate deposits. If I'm in a black mood, I'll probably adopt a curt negotiation style that'll be offensive.

If this happens, I know I'll come out on the short end of the stick and I'll grow angry with myself. I'll risk injuring some important relationships with vendors.

That could lead to my getting down on myself even more, and that could deepen and prolong my lowered productivity. So if I can delay the negotiations, I'll wait. It may be for a day, or even a week. But the pause will truly refresh me and give me time to regroup, mentally and emotionally.

Buddhists have a saying:

"Waiting Is . . ."

I came across it long ago, and, frankly, I didn't have a clue as to what it meant! But now I take it to mean that waiting is often better than jumping right back into the action. I realize this cuts against our grain in America where many of us perceive effectiveness associated with doing instead of just being.

In fact, not doing is villianized and blamed for many of our negative conditions. It gets a really bad rap. But sometimes, as former California Governor Jerry Brown pointed out, "Not doing anything is the highest form of action."

An ancient Chinese book of wisdom asks:

"Can you be still and wait until your mud settles?"

This phrase makes me imagine that when I'm in a slump it's like being submerged in a muddy tank of water. If I flail about trying to break out of it, I'll only muddy the waters further.

If I wait long enough, the mud will descend to the bottom and the water will be clear. Then, I'll have a better chance to see where I am and where I need to go.

Desperation Simply Worsens Slumps

Have you ever watched a desperate gambler in action, say, at the Blackjack tables? He'll draw a hand and lose. On the next hand he'll double his bet to recover what he lost and to garner his hoped-for winnings.

But what if he loses the third hand? He might double the bet again while telling himself, "They can't beat me three times in a row!"

If the bettor is compulsive, he'll keep raising the stakes until both his money and credit run out. Usually, no one is there to convince him that he should sit out at least a few hands when the cards turn cold. If he can do nothing, he can conserve his assets to make a run at the tables later. Or, if he waits long enough, he might develop the wisdom to walk away entirely.

Ease Off When You Feel Yourself Pressing for Hits

My father had a theory. When most of us lose, we try to force ourselves into victories. We press.

When ballplayers press too hard, they strike out more than ever before. When salespeople press, we seem overly aggressive and hostile instead of easygoing and friendly.

We literally scare away business.

The Oath of Hippocrates, which physicians have taken for thousands of years contains a wise provision that we can all learn from. It doesn't require doctors to try to heal everyone, though this is what many people believe. It says:

"Don't knowingly do harm."

We could all put that idea to good use. If you suspect that by taking action you'll worsen things, don't act.

A Second Great Tip: Try Doing Something Mindless

There are some people who just can't do nothing. You may be one of them. So, the next tip might be a better idea for you.

The second approach to managing black moods is to do some mindless activity to keep your hands busy. Recently, I decided to clean a desk that was overflowing with undone items.

I hadn't pasted up my archival copies of the numerous articles that I had written for publications. So I quietly went about sifting through the magazines and newsletters until I came to those that I wanted to work on.

Before I realized it, an hour and a half had gone by and I had sorted and copied ten articles. I could see the beautiful golden oak finish of my desk, a sight that had been concealed from me for at least three months!

The payoffs from doing these minor things are dramatic. Now, I can choose from an array of reprints to mail and fax to sales prospects. By selecting suitable ones, I'll be more likely to earn business that will earn money and help me to feel good about myself.

I can also put together a portfolio of publications that may convince a syndicate to sell my articles on a national or international basis. That would create a larger audience for my ideas while producing a stream of income.

These mighty outcomes result from doing what seems to be mindless, clerical work.

By dropping tiny pebbles into ponds, you can produce waves and waves of benefits. The key to working out of a black mood this way is to not make yourself feel you have to move mountains. All you have to do is to lift little stones.

You actually might end up moving mountains, because the best way to go about it is by removing one stone at a time.

But let's get back to our gambler. He doesn't want to have anything to do with little pebbles. No, he feels he has to have instant, dramatic success to end his slump and stop his losses.

Don't Feel You Have to Swing for the Fences

The concept of having to exercise a master stroke that will smash through all resistance is problematic. It can lead to perfectionism and procrastination. I'll explain.

It's hard to ease yourself out of a slump if you think you have to produce an immediate, huge breakthrough. Slumpers secretly know that the odds of achieving instantaneous, phenomenal success are low.

Being short of patience, yet behind the eight-ball, we bet the farm, emotionally, instead of concentrating on making modest strides on the road to success.

We clutch for straws in desperation and fail. Feeling stigmatized by losing, we're less likely to try again, fearing that any and all attempts we make will be in vain.

So urgent and desperate moves can follow periods of delay and procrastination. When these spasms don't produce for us, we retreat just as quickly and forcefully. We become more deeply mired in a cycle of failure and despair. That's when major-league slumps envelop us.

A Final Great Tip: Try Doing Something Entirely NEW!

A third tactic is available to dig us out of the depths. We can try entirely new strategies instead of pressing on with those that haven't been working for us. Modest investments in novel techniques can create big wins for us, if not in the present, than in the future.

One of my favorite expressions is this one:

One of the marks of unbalanced people is they keep doing the same things the same old way, but they expect to achieve different results!

If we want new outcomes, we need to use new techniques. Otherwise, we'll be like those toy trucks that keep bumping into the same wall without making suitable corrections.

Sometimes We Don't Notice We're Burned-Out

I taught college over a five-year period. When I began at age twenty-three, it was a real thrill. My ideas were respected, and the classroom was a fun place to be.

By twenty-eight, after I had earned my Ph.D., I wasn't totally burned out but I was on my way. Teaching just wasn't the kick it had once been.

I felt my lectures were growing stale, and I didn't have much interest in updating them. I had clearly lost the edge and the keen interest in excellence that I had embodied for the previous sixty months.

I devised an exit strategy so I could bridge to a new career. I designed a one-day seminar, which I asked Cal State Los Angeles to sponsor for me.

The course only drew six attendees, but they loved it. I took that as encouragement to keep on keepin on. I returned to Indiana, where I was teaching at DePauw University, and I phoned a number of other schools.

They agreed to run the class, and attendance shot up. The program became very popular, and within six months of having conducted the first one at C.S.U.L.A., I turned these one-day events into a full-time, profitable business.

But I can't emphasize too strongly how modest my beginnings were. I invested very little time outlining the class before I taught it the first time out. Granted, I had refined many of the units through my college teaching, but still, I started with a very modest innovation, and over a reasonably short period of time, it germinated into a great little business and a new career.

If I had become terribly ego-involved in making the continuing education venture work, I might have screwed up the entire deal. But because I fostered reasonable expectations, I was able to see encouragement where more seasoned seminar providers could have seen failure.

I suppose I was ready to make a new opportunity, so I simply tried something that was completely different, at least for me, and it worked!

Don't Snatch Defeat from the Clutches of Victory

When we're slumping, it's easy to get into a pattern where we snatch defeat from the jaws of victory. Unless we break attendance records with a new course or have staggering success with an initiative, we might tell ourselves that something's wrong!

It's not true. What might be needed are some minor adjustments. In my case, the Midwest was the fertile soil that I needed for my little sprout of a new business to grow. My class needed nurturing, and I'm grateful to schools such as Indiana State University that put up the seed money and helped me out.

A modest idea and a few sales to universities helped to pull me out of a career slump.

People who feel they need bigness in order to pull out of slumps are simply misleading themselves.

I know someone who opened a marketing firm about a year ago. He struggled and wasn't making much headway.

Instead of giving quality feedback to his clients to tell them how their projects were doing, he'd stall, which created frustration and exasperation.

He wasn't good at his job, and he insisted upon surrounding himself with people who were weaker still. On the verge of collapse, he found a new investor who bought a controlling interest in the firm.

Did things change with an infusion of new money? Not at all. It was attributable to the fact that the founder couldn't think small. He would envision great sales numbers, but he was personally incapable of closing the bread-and-butter deals that would pay the bills.

His undisputed strength was in getting investors to share his enthusiastic dreams of grandeur. I can tell you this: his slumps make the Grand Canyon look like a pothole!

Get to Know Your Bad Moods and Slumping Cycles

Compare the last example to a consulting client of mine. This fellow, along with a partner, has opened a financial services business that has great promise. The founders are an experienced team who have made a number of prior projects successful.

Despite their success and affluence, they both work exceedingly hard at developing a working routine for the new business that can become franchised to other business people later on.

No detail is too small for the bosses to pay close attention to and to master. They listen to my sales training tapes, again and again, to and from work while driving in the car.

They're completely immersed in their work and accountable for every outcome. And they're not too bloated in the head to step in occasionally to help their employees to close deals.

Do they have emotional ups and downs? You bet. Mitch, one of the partners admitted to me:

"I blow up every other day, but people get to know me and they realize I'm harmless."

Do you see how well he knows his cycles? Every other day he's a different person. Cheerful and optimistic one day. Down and dour the next.

There's nothing inherently wrong with this emotional see-saw, providing you're aware of the pattern and able to deal with it effectively.

I'm very cynical about certain people who say you can and should be completely happy-happy-happy all the time. If you were, you'd probably be something other than human.

We should be generous with ourselves and allow for the fact that some things will occasionally get out of hand.

Marvin Gaye, the Motown singer, echoed this Biblical suggestion in one of his songs:

"Change what you can; what you can't—leave it alone—and have the sense to know the difference between the two."

If you have a periodic slump cycle, recognize it. But don't let it throw you. Don't become afraid of the idea of having a slump. That fear itself could become debilitating.

It's as President Franklin Roosevelt said with respect to a similar concern: "The only thing we have to fear, is fear itself."

Give consideration to how you're going to respond to your setbacks and periodic slowdowns. There is an ancient tradition in Buddhism that supports the entire concept of relinquishing control by breaking our habit of caring so much about outcomes.

There is a similar notion in Judeo-Christian philosophy. When we "Let go, and let God," handle our problems, as churchman Robert Schuller has said, miraculous things happen, seemingly, by themselves.

In other words, we shouldn't try to micromanage our moods. We can't see or know the future, let alone control all earthly events. Appreciate that some processes are simply beyond our control, and then feel free to let go of the bad times and move on toward the good times!

Don't Fight Windmills

One of the most effective ways we have to work our way out of a slump is to make sure that we're fighting the right battles. Like Don Quixote, we often aim our anger at targets that are inappropriate like our spouses, customers, or pets. If we can simply channel unwanted emotions, whether in the form of anger, envy, or disappointment, then we'll certainly make plusses from our minuses.

When I was eleven, I was appointed to our Little League all-star team. Unfortunately, I was benched until we were losing a game by four runs and there were two outs in our last time at bat.

I was so mad at the manager for leaving me out that I balked when he said I should pinch hit for another player. What happened next was remarkable.

I walked into the batter's box and a few pitches that were balls went by. But I was so angry that I vowed to destroy the next round object that flew anywhere near the plate.

BOOM! I blasted a line-drive shot off the left field wall, which would have been a home run had it been hit a foot higher. As it turned out, it was a double that knocked in a run.

Our defeat wasn't nearly as dramatic, and I felt redeemed. But I also emerged from that event with the belief that if you channel your emotions in productive ways you can benefit greatly. I took out my anger on the ball.

Transform Your Fear into Eager Anticipation

Convert your emotions this way. Imagine being asked to sell to a large group. You're afraid because you've never addressed a gathering this size. You could waste your time and your emotional energy by saying, "I'll screw-up, I know it!"

Or, you could USE THE FEAR and turn it into EAGER ANTICIPATION.

Allow yourself to tingle with exhilaration. Interpret your butterflies as welcomed antecedents to success. When experienced actors are asked if they experience stage fright before performances they almost all reflexively say *of course!*

But they're veterans at channeling their fears into positive energy. They focus upon their roles and their lines. They walk themselves through their plays, scene after scene, and imagine audiences responding warmly.

Instead of dissipating your energy through anxiety and fear of failure, become a smart performer. Use these emotions constructively to turbocharge your work. It's just as easy to use your imagination to envision positive outcomes instead of negative ones.

Working Is Always Easier than Worrying

It's always easier to work than to worry. Worry accomplishes nothing unless we change our circumstances for the better. Once we take action, worry disappears. Someone once defined worry as:

Powerlessness projected into the future.

When we worry, we're really afraid that we won't perform capably at some date down the road. Of course, that could come true if we fail to prepare in a positive way. By worrying we end up procrastinating, and that prevents us from doing what we need to do in order to succeed. A vicious circle of worry and inactivity is ushered in. The more inactive we are, the more we worry; and that means we simply prolong our inactivity and subsequent concern.

Try setting up a new mental monitor to observe what you're thinking and what you're telling yourself. For example, I'll catch myself mentally saying, "I'm tired."

That may be accurate, but unless I summon energy, I'll want to take a nap or simply kick-back. So I challenge that thought when I hear it cropping up in my mind:

My blood sugar is wacko because I just ate a big lunch. Hang in there. Your energy will bounce back!

And it always does. If I give in to the random thoughts that occur, I'll relinquish control over my output and simply create more waste.

Overcoming Boredom

Some wise person once said, "If you're bored, it's your own fault."

Boredom is generally a useless emotion unless we perceive it as a signal that we're talking ourselves into a funk.

We can make boredom pay off, if we try. I suggest you try to transform your boredom into a different emotion: *disgust.*

When I'm disgusted I act with boldness and tremendous resolution. It's like I'm gunning the motor and just about to blast past the starting line in a race.

It doesn't matter that I don't know exactly where I'm going to go. All I know is I'm GOING SOMEWHERE and I'm going there any second! This feeling of impending thrust is a whole heck of a lot better than going nowhere languishing in boredom.

If we grow disgusted with boredom or inactivity, we can devise a plan to overcome it. And here's the good news: By the time our plan is underway we will have forgotten about our boredom!

Try Accomplishing Just One More Thing

Abe Lincoln once said:

"I walk slowly, but I never have to go back."

You may find that you're feeling sluggish, and you're tempted to chuck things for the day. Try the following:

Do just one more thing before you call it a day.

It could be tossing out a direct mail piece you received that you felt ambivalent about. It's a good time to chuck it and to make space for more important things.

Make a list of tomorrow's activities. By getting organized now you'll save time floundering about wondering what your priorities are when tomorrow arrives. List making is a calming activity that is done best when you're winding down.

The end of the day is a good time to reflect and review your accomplishments. I carry a writing tablet with me when I'm having a meal out and when I'm waiting for a movie to begin at a theater.

Instead of gawking at other people or the decor I'm getting things done and making notes of the new ideas that are popping in to my mind. By the same token, if I'm not reading a magazine when standing in line at the supermarket, I feel that I've wasted a major opportunity.

I don't mean to suggest that I have a chance to digest meaty articles, but I broaden my awareness of people and events when I pick up errant publications. It's stimulating and encourages the creative process.

By exposing myself to ideas that are outside of my ordinary frame of reference I stand a good chance of having those ideas, and my familiar ones, merge into novel combinations. Wasted time becomes productive time.

One of my consulting clients produces a multitasking software product that enables a user to work in a number of open applications at once. I've always liked the idea of multitasking because the term suggests that we can accomplish multiple things at the same time.

We can multitask if we teach ourselves how to do it. For example, I can write almost any time and any place despite the presence of distractions that would drive others nuts. This is a learned skill.

If you grew up in a large family, you probably did your homework while your siblings were carrying on, shouting, and jumping around. If so, you already may have the right wiring to multitask.

To test your capabilities, try reading a book when you're sitting at a bus stop at a crowded intersection. Can you effectively block out the traffic noise as well as the potentially distracting presence of other people and concentrate on the book? If not, work on it as an exercise in flexible concentration.

We waste time, not in major chunks, but in little tidbits. To turn these losses into gains, we need to seize them as they present themselves, or manufacture them where they don't seem to be present.

Occasionally, when I'm conducting a seminar I'll assign the task of writing a script. While my attendees are doing this, I'll take the opportunity to write something of my own, relevant to the course or to some other objective.

I'm there for them to handle any questions that arise, but I'm also there for me and for a number of auxiliary tasks that wait in the wings to be done.

There is a direct relationship between how you utilize your time and the frequency and severity of the slumps you experience. Slumps often happen when you feel you aren't accomplishing enough.

By finding constructive actions for dead times we gain a powerful sense of accomplishment. We're getting a lot done, and we know it. Small gains lead to larger ones, and before long, we've built up a head of steam that can pull us, like a locomotive, out of a slump.

We need to create a sense of abundance and affluence to stay on the right track. If we can do those things that make us feel we're ahead of the game, then we can sustain that feeling. Small gains do the trick, because at the end of the day we can see that we've done a surprising number of things.

Once we feel good about ourselves, we can then take on more challenging tasks. And our odds of finishing them in fine form are enhanced.

A body in motion tends to stay in motion, and a body at rest tends to remain at rest.

It's a law of physics, and it's a psychic law as well. When we're winning we tend to keep on winning. The trick is to find a way to win, in baby steps, instead of in giant leaps. Remember:

Inch by inch, it's a cinch. Yard by yard, it's hard.

In business, there are several ways to turn waste into treasure. How many of us turn our losses into gains by understanding why we failed?

Knock Out Your Time Wasters

One major slump-busting activity is to work on eliminating time wasters. A great way to begin is by keeping a log of your activities.

The goal isn't to root out all of the joy in your calendar or to fill every minute with hectic activities. What you want to do is to assign the best times of the day to accomplishing certain activities.

For instance, I like to write in the early morning. It serves two goals for me.

1. I'm able to produce a meaningful, measurable result at the start of day. That makes me feel good about myself.

2. Writing is actually a great way to wake up and to dust off the mental cobwebs.

My mind may still be half asleep, but when my ideas start to flow, I leave drowsiness behind. Writing in the morning is also a peaceful, contemplative activity, and that suits my personality.

I'm just not very talkative in the early a.m.!

So, while others in my family are sleeping, I'm making hay and I like that a lot. It's amazing how much writing I can get accomplished in an hour or two every morning.

If I have a chance to do more later in the day or in the evening, that's an added bonus. I feel that I'm getting ahead of the game.

Right now, I'm listening to a new salesman make phone calls to sell my audio programs to businesses. It's his first day at it, so I don't want to hover. But he still needs to know that I'm involved, which I am, so I'm stationed about fifteen feet from him in my office with my door wide open.

I can write and monitor his progress at the same time. What makes it possible is the fact that he dials and communicates in spurts, and I write the same way.

When I hear him begin a new call, I slow down and listen for anything unusual. If all is well, I keep on writing.

If I concentrated exclusively on him at this moment, it would be wasteful. But by performing two tasks at the same time, I'm gaining ground on both fronts.

Enroll in the Rolling University: Your Car

For many commuters, driving time is wasted time, and it is also frustrating. Why not turn those miles and bumper-to-bumper jams into gold?

You can do it by becoming an audio junkie. I listen to tapes to learn languages and to expose myself to positive ideas. There are some tapes that I've listened to a hundred times because I find them so uplifting.

They never grow old for me, because I get something out of them every time. It's a lot more productive than listening to talk radio.

Reduce Slump Time by Getting Back to Your Success Script

As a sales manager and consultant, I have trained thousands of salespeople. They're almost all a pleasure to work with when they're new to the job and they're green. Trainees, generally, make a real effort to follow my directions to the letter.

When they do, they sell very well and succeed quickly, but after they've tasted the first fruits of success, they'll stray from the presentation I just struggled so hard to teach them. They'll usually substitute a freeform, improvised pitch in its place. Their sales will tank, and they'll be genuinely befuddled as to why they've fallen into a slump.

They'll attribute their lower sales to anything other than the fact that they have changed their sales routines. If I'm coaching them, I'll observe them while they sell, and it'll be an easy matter to say, "Hey, get back to your planned presentation!"

Novices will generally be grateful for the advice. But what happens when I'm dealing with seasoned naturals? Are they as easy to coach back into success and prosperity? Not really.

One of the problems of naturals is that they seldom deliberately use a formatted presentation. I say deliberately because most of them ARE SCRIPTED, but they don't realize it because they've never stopped to record or to write down what they say, when they usually say it, and how they say it.

When they're slumping, it's not easy for them to return to a baseline performance that they are aware of, which can assure them of achieving at least minimal success. And naturals usually reject the entire concept of mechanically working themselves out of their slumps.

This might be the best thing to do when one's improvised approach fails. Try getting back to basics.

Think of yourself as a machine, a robot that is going to program itself to only perform those movements that contribute to sales outcomes.

This won't be easy, because there seem to be some built-in problems humans have with repeating sales behaviors.

A Revealing Experiment

An experiment was performed that supports the idea that it is difficult for people to stick to scripts because they grow bored with unchanging routines—even if these routines consistently make sales for them.

John Lilly, an Ivy League psychologist, asked subjects to go into a listening room with a tape recorder. They were asked to note on a piece of paper every word they heard coming from the machine.

Lilly gave each person a notepad with sixty spaces to enter the words. A single word was uttered by the machine every fifteen seconds for fifteen minutes, so the pace was reasonable.

When people turned in their pads with the answers that they had written, the experimenters saw lots of different words on each pad.

This was curious because all of the subjects heard the SAME WORD repeated sixty times. Had they listened accurately, they would have written down the identical word in each space on their pads.

Lilly concluded that people respond much less like machines than psychologists once thought. We don't passively accept each stimulus we encounter and imprint it accurately upon our minds.

We often reshape it as we're experiencing it as if we're molding plastic items with our minds. Lilly said people act like a hybrid of machine and organism. He calls us biocomputers.

We're like computers in some respects, but we have an irrepressible need to manipulate our experiences and to not reproduce the same exact experience twice.

I believe that's why natural born salespeople often rebel against using a written presentation the same way over and again, despite the fact that it could put money into their pockets if they simply make themselves repeat it.

This Is the Other Place

This need for variety reminds me of a great episode of the "Twilight Zone." A gangster is gunned down during a robbery, and, suddenly, he discovers he is being transported to the afterlife by a guide.

The guide tells the gangster that he can have anything he likes. The bad guy says he wants to play Blackjack. Donning a green visor, the guide deals the cards.

Every hand gives the gangster 21—an instant winner. Tiring of the monotony of never losing, the stickup artist says he wants to shoot pool. Instantly, a table appears and the guide racks the balls. With a single shot the criminal gets all of the balls into the pockets. He grumbles, "Rack 'em up, again!" The guide does so, and the same thing happens. All the balls fly into the pockets. The shooter can't miss.

Finally, in frustration the criminal declares, "If this is your idea of Heaven, I don't like it at all. I want to go to the other place!" Coldly, the guide informs him, "This IS the other place."

Even if we could function like machines, and produce neat, perfect sales every time, would we want to?

Theoretically, that would make us super rich, but it could also be boring. As in the "Twilight Zone," it could feel like a living Hell.

It's possible that our genetic makeup compels us to seek variety as a survival mechanism. We have such large cerebral cortexes that we're capable of inventing new scenarios, which may enable us to cope with changing circumstances, but also induce us to paint ourselves into slumps because we're bored with success.

Maintaining an evenly balanced emotional disposition and repeating the same routines, however successful, may not be in the biological cards for salespeople.

For the purpose of emerging faster from slumps, naturals may have to bridle themselves and use a disciplined sales routine until the time comes when their sales are soaring once more.

Don't Be Afraid to Lose a Job or to Change Jobs

As a consultant for the last seventeen years, I've experienced at least a few lulls in activity. I've often thought of my between consulting assignment periods as opportunities. Not as frequent troughs when no revenue is coming in, but as a respite from a routine that may have grown stale.

When I sell a contract to a client, it's closed ended. We know when I'm going to start and when I'm going to finish. This sort of definiteness is actually relieving to everyone.

Fostering the illusion of permanent employment, most workers perceive separations and terminations as unnatural events. Things to be mourned. But I don't, because if I did, I'd always be wearing black! Hellos and good-byes simply come along with the territory if you're a consultant.

Just to dramatize the different attitudes you can have toward work, let me share a story with you. When I was about to finish my Ph.D., I started a job search.

I attended two conventions in my field, and I interviewed for the most promising positions. Everyone, including me, was seeking a full-time, tenure-track teaching position. This meant that you'd be hired with the expectation that you'd try to earn lifetime employment by performing well during a six-year probationary period. If your colleagues and the college's administration thought well of your teaching and research, they'd vote to give you tenure. After that, you could be aboard forever.

I received a tenure-track position with a fine liberal arts college, but after the initial elation wore off, I experienced a very different emotion.

Do I really want to work here for the next thirty to forty years?

That thought was chilling! How boring! How stagnant! After one academic year, I resigned.

Many of us seek permanence and a feeling of security only to find that when we have it these guarantees don't assure the satifactions we anticipated.

The same teaching position that made me feel a surge of success when I first landed the job also ushered in a feeling of impending doom. It represented the best of times and the worst of times.

That's human, feeling the highs and the lows, the gains and the losses. They're a part of having a full life. If you're between sales jobs, don't worry. You're heading towards something bigger and better—believe me!

Be Grateful for What You DO Have

Recently, I saw an interview with an athlete who permanently lost the use of his legs. Every morning he wakes up and is starkly reminded that his mobility is restricted. Then, he says he makes up his mind to accomplish great things, nonetheless.

His loss is huge, but he wastes as little time as he can bemoaning his circumstances. He even uses his disability as positive motivation by telling himself that he can achieve even more than people who still have their mobility.

Another paraplegic who was also featured in the program decided to open a business that combines his disability with his fondness for bicycles. The result is a business that manufactures special wheelchairs that he has personally designed. They're successful because they've been built from the point of view of their users.

Do What You Can with What You Have

I was just reading a review of a novel, *Dog Eat Dog*. It was written by a prison inmate who has spent over twenty-five years behind bars. He started writing when he learned that a famous fellow inmate, Caryl Chessman, had published a book.

Not to be outdone, Edward Bunker started writing in prison, and through a lot of hard work he became a successful writer. He even acted in Quentin Tarantino's film, *Reservoir Dogs*.

Now he has enough film credits to earn him a pension from a film industry retirement fund. Mr. Bunker is a fine example of an individual who has learned to turn waste into treasure. Wouldn't you agree?

When you consider how many years are wasted through idle incarceration, it makes you wonder why our lockups don't produce more authors and journalists, as well as other important contributors to society.

A part of the problem is that people can't see the gold that lies beneath the surface—the surface of themselves. We don't realize our potential or the possibilities for making a quality use of the time or the resources we have.

A prisoner of war from the Vietnam era explained how he kept his sanity and his alertness amidst inhumane confinement. Every day he would play a round or two of golf. That is, he'd play the game in his mind. He'd awaken in the morning, mentally put on his gear, travel to the course, and then have the time of his life.

Every shot he hit was flawless. He never missed putting the ball into the cup. He reconstructed every blade of grass, every hole, and each view of the course from all angles.

This active use of imagination kept his hope alive, and it was the very best use of his time. By the time he actually played on a real course after he was repatriated, his golf game was excellent.

All of that mental practice, assisted by an active imagination, helped him to recover his sport and his life.

We can do exactly the same thing when we're in a selling slump. Imagine that you're about to make the best sales presentations of your life. Picture in your mind grateful prospects who are nodding in appreciation as you speak. Envision their delight in approving your proposals. Propel yourself into the future, see their elation and willingness to serve as excellent references and sources of new business.

Change Your Attitude Toward Slumps

If we can't avoid having slumps, we can certainly adjust our attitudes about them. We can choose to view them as constructive and productive periods in our careers.

Try relishing them. Think of them as time-outs—neither good or bad—just intervals when we can catch our breath and experience something different.

How Naturals Learn to Turn Waste into Treasure

Slumps are an utter waste of time and human resources from most people's perspectives. After all, we're not making sales when we're stuck, so what good are they?

Naturals have a different take on the significance of slumps. They might say:

"One person's junk is another person's fortune."

Look at any auto graveyard and you'll see what I mean. Old carcasses of steel and upholstery litter the landscape. These items look like the discards of the desperate, and, in many cases, they are. They're the ruins of our mobile society. But the used auto parts dealer knows that there's treasure in that waste.

A hard to find side mirror for a 1987 Thunderbird can fetch well above $75. That's when a motivated owner can even locate one.

It's a matter of supply and demand. The junk dealer knows that when someone needs a rare item, he'll be paid handsomely for going to the trouble of stocking the item.

Our recycling movement, which is becoming a staple in communities across America, is an outgrowth of the same positive thinking about seemingly useless items. As a recent television commercial says, a plastic soda bottle can be recycled and replenished for a new customer within a matter of weeks.

The same kind of thinking can be used when it comes to profiting from our sales slumps. Epictetus, the ancient Greek known for a number of wise aphorisms, said:

It isn't the events, themselves, that disturb people. It's our attitudes about events that disturb us.

Rebuild, Brick By Brick

After the 1994 Northridge earthquake in California, a building I owned—for which I wasn't insured—suffered substantial damage. I had to have what remained demolished. I received several bids, and then I asked the lowest bidder a question:

"How much will you credit me if I let you keep the undamaged bricks?"

He didn't expect that question, despite the fact that used bricks fetch a pretty penny from people who buy them for their character, when remodeling patios and planting areas.

He gave me several hundred dollars for the bricks, which I used as a credit toward my repairs.

Those bricks had zero value to me. Actually, they had a negative value because I was thinking I'd have to pay someone to haul them away!

So I profited twice from having turned wasted materials into treasure. This is the kind of thinking that we should use to turn our selling setbacks into advancements.

How to Transform Lost Causes into Today's Sales

A few years ago, I failed to earn the business of a famous modeling agency. After speaking on the phone several times to my contact, I heard nothing.

Apparently, my proposal wasn't being given any further consideration. Instead of tossing aside the work I had put into cultivating the account, I decided to write them a note. I asked for feedback as to where we went wrong and how we failed.

Within a week I was contacted by a different official in the company, and a little later on she rewarded me with a national consulting contract. Persistence salvaged a lot of good preliminary work and helped me to turn waste into treasure.

Failing Is Temporary

There is a link between our sense of waste and fear of failing. If you earned an F in a class in school, what did you have to do?

You had to repeat the class. So the first time you took it was considered a waste, as if you sat in class during the entire term for nothing.

You did some work, but you had nothing to show for it but negative results. I think one of our problems in sensing underlying value in waste is the fact that we think its unredeemable. Once something is wasted, it's asset value is nil.

This isn't valid. Waste doesn't always create a total loss, unless we turn away from it without deriving some benefit. Let me give you an example of what I see as a waste in a business setting.

I hire people to sell my products. For years, I paid an hourly wage plus a bonus based upon results. Over that time I utilized very few people who really pushed themselves to achieve sales glory.

Most muddled through, and their work didn't give me much in the form of results. One day I visited a client who paid his people on a very different basis.

Instead of offering the arrangement I used, he paid his people on a straight commission basis. When they sold, they prospered. If they merely tried without producing results, they received no pay.

It sounds a little harsh, doesn't it? We're so used to receiving pay for effort that working on a pay-for-performance basis seems exceedingly onerous.

This is exactly what business owners do all the time. If they open restaurants and patrons don't materialize, they can't take big salaries out for themselves. It's unfortunate, but it's one of the risks of capitalism.

My client had aligned his interests with those of his employees. They were after the same thing: customers. If one won, the other won.

I tried it on as a compensation formula, but I found that very few people want to work on a straight commission basis. They realize that there is more money in it if they succeed, but they are gripped with a major fear:

They're afraid to waste their time and their effort.

If they worked hard but produced no sales, how would they rationalize their efforts to their friends, families, and mates? I realize that they could say, "I tried something, but it didn't work out for me."

That's not such a big admission, is it? Maybe, not for me, but it's major for most people. The stigma of failing, of having to repeat a course or finding another job where they can succeed, is traumatic.

But it shouldn't be that way.

How can anything be a waste if we've learned from it?

I provided each person I hired on a straight commission with training that she or he could take to the next job. It was first-class training that imparted new and useful skills. It had monetary value, and to the smart person it was well worth the time that they invested on-site with me.

I had a number of failures when I hired this way. Does that mean that my hiring technique was a waste? Not at all! I ended up hiring one person who had just what it took to succeed. But he had an ingredient that was missing from most: patience.

By hiring, training, and losing people before I recruited this fellow, I found out what the most important psychological trait is for individuals to succeed on a straight commission basis: patience.

This insight helped me weed out all kinds of folks who had the skills to achieve but the wrong mental attitude. Unless they could commit to giving my opportunity at least two weeks to work for them, I couldn't bring them aboard.

I ended up doing something that an old book of wisdom urges:

Always take a profit from your loss.

It's sad that most people in our culture are so quick to categorize their experiences as losses and complete wastes of time and energy. If they'd only go that extra step to cash in on what they've already invested, they'd realize how there's really no such thing as waste, unless we make it so.

Just yesterday I was reading about a mom who lost her daughter to violence in a far away land. The young woman had been working to promote election reforms in South Africa. Two days before she was scheduled to return to her Newport Beach, California home, she was slain for her participation in that political cause.

Now, a year later, mom has taken up her daughter's cause. She is striving to complete her child's mission. No words can express the sadness that the mother must feel over her loss, but she's turning it into something positive for herself and an entire country.

When you feel you're entering or you're stuck in a slump, ask yourself what good can come from this. What can I do, right here and now, that will turn what appears to be waste into treasure?

Just by asking that question you will have already begun the solution.

AFTERWORD

If you want to sell like a natural born salesperson, try putting the advanced techniques you've learned from this book to work.
Remember to:

1. Maintain high self-esteem so that you always feel you deserve the sale.
2. Create instant credibility and rapport with your prospects.
3. Get your customers to sell themselves.
4. Use passion and powerful emotions when selling.
5. Persuade by employing effective body language.
6. Multiply your impact by mastering several sales media while never wasting your time.
7. Turn lemons into lemonade by transforming every setback, rejection, and slump into a major advantage.

Do these things again and again, and I assure you that you'll have a great time and enjoy a rich and gratifying career.

TO CONTACT
THE AUTHOR

Thank you for reading my book. I hope it will have a positive impact on your income and your working life.

I'd enjoy hearing from you if you'd like to share some of your sales war stories, or learn about obtaining some of my other books, audio, or video programs. I also speak at sales meetings, deliver on-site training seminars, and consult in the areas of sales skills and sales management, telephone selling, and customer service.

I can be reached at the following address:

Dr. Gary S. Goodman
P.O. Box 9733
Glendale, CA 91226
phone: (818) 243-7338, (818) 244-8355
fax: (818) 956-2242
e-mail: salesdoc@earthlink.net

Good Luck!

INDEX